DEMOCRACY
ALL THAT MATTERS

DEMOCRACY

Steven Beller

ALL THAT MATTERS

ALL THAT MATTERS

Contents

1 Introduction: Why should we care about democracy? 1

2 What do we mean by 'democracy'? 13

3 Where did democracy come from? Forms of government 25

4 Where else did democracy come from? The rule of law, the state and civil society 37

5 Where has democracy got to lately? Community and diversity 51

6 How does democracy work? 65

7 How democratic are our democracies? 79

8 Can democracy work beyond the nation-state? 95

9 Is there a future for democracy? 109

10 Conclusion: Why we should
care about democracy   125

100 Ideas   137

Index   149

Acknowledgements   154

Introduction: Why should we care about democracy?

'If we just scratch the surface a little in the established democracies, the complacency that prevails there soon appears unwarranted.'

ALL THAT MATTERS

It might seem quite redundant to ask why we should care about democracy. Most of the people who read this book will be living in a democracy, or at least in a state that claims to be one. Most of them will go about their business every day not giving much thought to the democratic institutions by which their lives are governed. They will assume that the political arrangements involved are not going to change much any time soon and, despite the occasional gripe, that they are more or less acceptable, and certainly not worth fighting over when there are better things in life to be concerned with and to strive for. Democracy is a given in their lives, whether or not they think it performs well for them or not – in fact, their form of democracy performs well enough to make them relatively unconcerned about what that democracy actually consists of, where it is heading, or even whether it needs their help in order for it to thrive or survive.

There might be many causes that still rouse the public of the Western democracies to activism, to demonstrate, and to donate their time and money, but democracy itself, generally speaking, is not one of them. This seems to be the obvious conclusion of the decline in percentages of the electorate voting in elections over the last few decades, and the falling away from traditional political parties. Complacency, even apathy – not commitment – appears to be the dominant attitude.

▶ Democracy in the ascendancy?

There are good, empirical reasons why people living in democracies today might think that they need do little, if anything, to keep them going – as democracies. The greatest threats to democracy have been on the retreat since the middle of the twentieth century. The anti-democratic Axis Powers of National Socialist Germany, fascist Italy and imperial Japan were defeated in 1945 and subsequently transformed into democracies. Quasi-fascist dictatorships that suppressed democratic movements in the developing world – and also in southern Europe – have largely been replaced by regimes that at least claim to adhere to democratic standards, and many of them are recognized by other democracies as such. In 1989 the world of Soviet-dominated communism, which saw itself as an opponent of at least *Western*-style democracy, collapsed. Most of the states of the former communist world have been transformed into democracies, or at least states claiming democratic status – not least Russia itself. Further revolutionary change in states such as South Africa and Indonesia in the 1990s brought more states into the community of democracies. In sub-Saharan Africa there has been an encouraging trend as countries such as Ghana and Nigeria have returned to democratic rule, with successive elections determining the transfer of power. The Arab Spring of 2011 has furthered this trend, leaving relatively few states that do not at least pretend to being democracies.

The current Community of Democracies, an international organization founded in 2000 to strengthen the global democratic cause, currently has over a hundred participants, and one example of the success of global democratization is that the current presiding state in the Community of Democracies is Mongolia. The Democracy Index of 2010 from the Economist Intelligence Unit had 78 full or 'flawed' democracies, and another 36 'hybrid regimes' that might still be classed as democratic – along with another 53 'authoritarian regimes' that could not be (despite what they might claim). Freedom House currently lists 117 out of the world's 195 nation-states as 'electoral democracies', which makes 60 per cent of the total. As recently as 1989 the equivalent figure was 69 out of 167, only 41 per cent. The significant expansion of democratic government across the globe in the last three decades might explain some of the public's complacency concerning democracy.

That still leaves a substantial number of countries where there is either no democracy, or only a limited form of it. The Democracy Index of 2010 listed only 25 out of 167 countries as full democracies, a mere 15 per cent of the world's countries, and covering only 11 per cent of the world's population. Even including 'flawed democracies' only bumps this up to 48 per cent of the world's population living under something properly called democracy. According to the Democracy Index, (just) over half the world's population still lives in countries that do not merit the democratic tag. Some major countries have been slipping backwards of late. Russia used to be seen as a hybrid regime, but is now classed by the Democracy Index as an authoritarian regime. (Freedom House concurs in seeing Russia as 'not free'.) Western democratic complacency would therefore appear to be misplaced. It all depends on how you read the figures and define what counts as a democracy – other measures are more optimistic. Nonetheless, there is still, in 2013, a long way to go before the world truly is 'safe for democracy'.

The places where there is the most enthusiasm for democracy today are those countries where democracy has not yet arrived, such as Burma, or those where it is still trying to get a firm foothold, such as Egypt. In such countries' populations there is little of the complacency found in established, 'safe' democracies, precisely because the presence and efficacy of the democratic system is, clearly, not so self-evident or unchallenged. Democracy appears to be something you really care for most in its absence. There might be a honeymoon period, but once you have had it for a time there seems little reason to care about it – or so history seems to show.

▶ An unwarranted complacency

The recent experience of the Arab Spring has shown that it takes a great deal of struggle, effort and also persuasion to overcome and replace non-democratic systems with recognizably democratic ones. One problem is that democracy is rarely the only option for replacing the old regime, and it is often unclear which is the truly democratic path. In Egypt the verdict is still out as to whether the army's dismissal of the democratically elected, but Islamist-dominated, Morsi government in July 2013 destroyed the democratic process begun in Tahrir Square, or saved it from destruction at the hands of anti-democratic religious fundamentalism. In Syria the cause of democracy appears to have been all but lost in what has become an increasingly vicious civil war – only time will tell if some form of democracy can emerge from this chaotic conflict. As we speak, people are fighting for democracy, but it is not clear that they are all fighting for the same thing; nor is it clear in many of these instances that they are winning. It bears repeating: over half the world's population still lives in countries that, under well-respected definitions, do not qualify as democracies.

▲ A democratic future?: demonstrators in Tahrir Square, Cairo, during the 2011 Egyptian revolution

If we just scratch the surface a little in the established democracies, the complacency that prevails there soon appears unwarranted. In Europe there is currently much frustration with the functioning of democratic institutions, especially on the transnational level of the European Union. Discussions about the 'democratic deficit' have been going on for many years, concerning the fact that the European Union is a union of governments rather than peoples, with no effective, Europe-wide democratic control of the 'Eurocrats' in Brussels. In the last few years, however, this low-level dissatisfaction has been brought to boiling point by the euro crisis, which has severely tested the collective resolve, and the power, of the governments of the Union to keep their finances afloat. The financial crisis has brought down a string of national governments within the Union, including Ireland, Spain, Portugal, Italy and, most notoriously, Greece. It has at times tested the ability of democratic systems to manage financial survival, and it has brought into question the relationship of the power of the people (democracy) with the power of the financial markets (plutocracy) in ways few would have thought possible in Europe a decade ago.

The current sense is that the worst is over, but many remain deeply unhappy about both their national governments and the effect of the European Union and its leading members on their economic wellbeing. Germany might be praised by some for providing the framework and capital for a new, more integrated European financial system, eventually, but it is also detested by large swathes of southern Europe for its ungenerous, nationally selfish approach to a European problem. If there was a 'democratic deficit' in Europe before the euro crisis, there are many now in the southern European states who doubt there is any democracy at all when it comes to European affairs, and precious little that democracy can do even at home to counter foreign, moneyed interests. Europhobic nationalism is also on the rise, most notably in Viktor Orbán's Hungary. All is not well in democratic Europe.

On the other side of the Atlantic, American democracy is not faring all that well either. The Supreme Court selected the President in 2001, after the very closely contested Bush vs. Gore election had been left hanging by a hanging chad. The reaction to the terrorist attack of 11 September 2001 led to a serious curtailment of many of the civil liberties of which Americans were justly proud. The election of Barack Obama as the first African American to be President in 2008 was a remarkable milestone, but so was, in its own way, the Supreme Court's ruling in the *Citizens United* case, which gave virtually free rein to corporations and the wealthy to pay for political propaganda *anonymously*. The full effect of this ruling was felt in the mid-term elections of 2010. These elections often favour the party out of power, but the stunning gains of the Republicans in the elections to the House of Representatives were greatly aided by the vastly disproportionate funding their candidates and political allies enjoyed due to *Citizens United.*

Immense efforts by the Democrats to come near to matching Republican fundraising for the 2012

Presidential election, and a poor Republican candidate in Mitt Romney, did result in the re-election of Obama (by a margin of about 3.8 per cent). The selection of severely right-wing candidates by the Republicans in several Senate races also led to more Democrats being elected to the Senate than had been thought possible a few months earlier. To that extent, the huge funding advantage of the right wing – for instance Karl Rove's Crossroads organization – did not achieve its potential, but it did mean that the election was probably closer than it would have been without *Citizens United* and in the House of Representatives the Republicans retained their majority quite comfortably, with only minor losses. The funding advantage explains part of this, but the striking fact is that Democratic House candidates received a million more votes from the electorate than their Republican counterparts did, with only two parties competing. Things being equal, the Democrats should have won the House as well, but things were not equal, because enough Republican-dominated state governments (the result of 2010) had gerrymandered their states' electoral districts to ensure a large Republican advantage. In Pennsylvania, Democrats had more votes (about 80,000 more) than Republicans, but took only 5 of the 18 House seats allotted to the state, with the Republicans walking away with 13.

Perhaps such malfunctioning of the US democratic process would not be so bad if other aspects were working well. The sort of mechanical voting problems that proved so fatal in the 2000 election did reoccur, but without the same impact, because the election was not quite so close.

Much more worrisome is that the party that profited most from the funding disequilibrium and from the rigging of electoral districts, the Republicans, is also dominated at this time by Tea Party right-wing ideologues who have an overtly confrontational understanding of how the American democratic system works, and little interest in compromise. The constant game of 'fiscal chicken' that now passes for democratic politics in America is seriously impairing the ability of the most powerful democracy in the world to function properly.

There are brighter spots in the democratic community at the moment. The economic growth of India and Brazil has boosted those countries' democratic characters as well. In the summer of 2013 demonstrations in Brazil, calling for less corruption and more effective public services, can be seen as a positive sign of this democratization. The same might be said about recent demonstrations in Turkey, and the overall positive democratic record in the Muslim-majority states of Turkey and Indonesia also offers hope that the supposed 'clash of civilizations' between a theocratic Islam and a democratic West is more a mind-cramp of academics on the neo-conservative Right in America than an inevitable political reality.

▶ Alternative models

On the other hand, the most successful economy in the world today in terms of growth is the People's Republic of China. With roughly 20 per cent of the world's population (approximately 1.4 billion), China is soon slated to be also the world's *largest* economy. Its leaders portray their communist system, in reality a form of dirigiste oligarchy, as a more effective alternative to Western democracy. Others in the developing world, and even some in the developed world, look to the Chinese model as either superior to Western democracy, or at least as having many lessons to offer. If China's communist ideology is too much to swallow, there is also the more Western, but non-democratic, model of Singapore, a sort of neoliberal authoritarian regime that gets the job done, and runs society humanely and efficiently, from above.

The economic success of these non-democratic models, and the large capital resources that China has amassed in recent years, have lent them both prestige in the developing world, and in China's case has led to a vast increase of economic and hence political influence in many African states. If one also remembers that the state with the largest petroleum reserves is an absolute theocratic monarchy, Saudi Arabia, unlikely to change much in the near term, and the country with the second largest nuclear arsenal is 'not free' Russia, then it is clear that democracy has not entirely seen off its ideological or geopolitical rivals (friendly or otherwise). Democracy might be in the ascendant, but it is not as secure a governing principle as some might think. It is malfunctioning in many of its most established centres, and it still faces challenges from apparently viable alternative systems. There is a lot to concern us about democracy, even in 2013.

That democracy is not as simple or effective a governing system as we would like it to be is not a new insight.

Winston Churchill, notoriously, made the point in an Armistice Day speech in the House of Commons in 1947: 'No one pretends that democracy is perfect or all-wise. Indeed, it has been said that democracy is the worst form of government except all those other forms that have been tried from time to time.' And there is the rub. We might not have much respect for the democratic process – when it works we might ignore it, and when it does not work we might harbour grudges against it – but it turns out that it is – *by far* –the best system available.

The purpose of this book is thus not only to act as a guide to the career, character and reality of democracy. It is also to show that we definitely ought to care about democracy, because this being the least bad system available is not the mere product of happenstance, or of practical experience. Rather, it is a fundamental, one might say self-evident, truth in the political and moral universe we inhabit in the modern age. Some form of what we call democracy is the best way of achieving the common good of all on a moral basis, now and in the future.

As a start, it would help if we knew what we were actually talking about: What do we mean by democracy?

2

What do we mean by 'democracy'?

'Neither freedom nor equality can ever be the universal principle of a society without the other – democracy lies in the field of tension between the two.'

The Chambers Dictionary defines 'democracy' primarily as 'a form of government in which the supreme power is vested in the people collectively, and is administered by them or by officers appointed by them' (which is fair enough, if ambivalent), and gives subsidiary meanings that emphasize the idea of commonality and political, social and legal equality. The most famous definition of democracy in America was that given at Gettysburg on 19 November 1863 by Abraham Lincoln, when he resolved that 'government of the people, by the people, for the people, shall not perish from the earth'. That will serve as a sound base, although the question as to who or what 'the people' is has had many answers over the ages. Lincoln's definition also does not say how this government of, by and for the people is to be instituted. To put it in the words attributed (falsely) to James Madison: 'How best are we to govern ourselves?' It is easy enough to say that people should be empowered to govern themselves. It has proven a far more difficult task to figure out how they can, theoretically and practically, do so: What are the necessary components of a democratic political system that make self-government by the people possible?

▶ The components of democracy

The current answer to that question, and hence what we usually mean when we use the word 'democracy', takes us, paradoxically, a long way from the seemingly simple idea of popular self-government. When the Community of Democracies, Freedom House or the Economist Intelligence Unit measure degrees of democracy in today's states and nations, they do so with criteria only a few of which are directly involved with questions of government of and by the people. Instead, 'democracy' as practised today involves:

- individual rights
- the rule of law
- protection of minorities
- the acceptance of diversity
- gender and racial equality before the law
- transparency of governmental and other public institutions
- good governance and accountability

to name just a few of the more prominent requirements. There are core elements that still reflect a more classically democratic content: popular sovereignty, majority rule, governmental responsibility (literally answerability) to the electorate. The following holds true for all modern-day democracies: If an individual or set of individuals is elected by a majority of the people to exercise its sovereignty in its name, they should at some point be required to go back to the people to answer for their government's record, and either be approved to continue, or be replaced by another individual or set of individuals. To that extent the people, or its elected representatives, still rule; otherwise it is not a democracy.

Yet this is just a base, and the additions and refinements that we automatically assume should be built on it greatly change the character of what we mean by democracy.

Partly, these accretions could be explained as being necessary due to recent experience with elections and democracy. There are many historical examples, going back at least to the French Revolution, if not further, but the negative experience of the fragility of the electoral process in the twentieth century has been especially marked. The peaceful, legal transfer of power in democratic systems to anti-democratic regimes, as occurred most notoriously in Germany in 1933, and the frequent failure of democratic systems in the post-colonial world, often with an elected government then eschewing the necessity of further democratic niceties, has led theorists and practitioners of democracy and democratization to adopt stringent measures to ensure that the first election in a new democracy is not its last. Robert A. Dahl, for instance, generates a substantial list of necessary conditions simply in order to ensure the survival of any representative democratic system: free, fair and frequent elections; freedom of expression; alternative information (free media); 'associational autonomy' (freedom of association); and inclusive citizenship. He also mentions elsewhere the conditions favouring democracy including control over the police and military and a growing market economy, as well as the desirability of the rule of law. If you add in the need for the population to have a democratic civic education so that they can exercise their democratic rights effectively, then the conditions simply for ensuring the successful launch of an 'electoral democracy' that will not stumble at the first electoral fence but rather be able to proceed to the second one and many thereafter – the paraphernalia of modern democracy – are already quite substantial in terms of their demands on any political or social system.

What we commonly ask of a 'full' democracy goes far beyond this election-guaranteeing minimum, however. Just as the European Union requires a new member to take on the now very substantial accumulation of laws and regulations (known as the 'Community acquis') that its membership has built up over the decades, so too, to a more limited but still considerable extent, does a state wanting to become a full-fledged democracy have to take on the rules and practices that the established democracies have accumulated, and these are much more than merely what is required to run a reasonable election. It usually requires a guarantee of property rights and a legal structure that will adequately protect those rights. It will also include a guarantee of freedom of movement, freedom of religion, freedom of association, and an equality before the law that is far more fundamental than merely a way of guaranteeing a fair and free election. Indeed, any democracy worth its name has to abide by a whole raft of human rights, as embodied in the United Nations Universal Declaration of Human Rights of 1948, and many subsequent human rights treaties and protocols, which inherently mean a great diminution of that state's power over its population. In other words, modern democracies are as much about the limiting of government power over its populace, even if that people is theoretically the sovereign of that government.

▶ Qualifiers of democracy

The main reason for all these freedoms and rights within modern democracy, which actually limit the power of the people within it, is that the liberal concept of representative, constitutional and *limited* government is prior to the concept of democracy, both historically and logically, within the modern Western political tradition, the main source of modern democracy. When we say 'democracy' we are in effect using a shorthand expression for 'liberal democracy'.

Liberal democracy is not the only qualifier for democracy – there are many different versions and varieties of the principle. Some of these have to do with the simple question of range, method or function. Hence ancient Greek democracy was a form of direct democracy, where the members of the polis took direct votes on what should be done. Some Swiss cantons still operate today with this method, and some townships in New England still exercise a residual form at town meetings. But generally speaking modern democracies, because of the numbers and distances involved, and the exigencies of the modern economy, are *representative* democracies, where the electorate elects representatives, who are the ones who actually vote on policy decisions. Referenda and ballot measures in various American states (and also in many European states) are attempts to replicate the direct popular control of direct democracy, but the popular will is mostly shown by voting for 'representatives', 'delegates' or 'deputies' to vote in legislative assemblies, or presidents and chancellors to exercise executive power, representing the popular will.

Some other 'democracies'

Local democracy refers to popular decision-making at the communal level; *federal* democracy to multi-layered structures of political power where sovereignty is split between regional states within the federal whole and between the federal and the regional state level.

Parliamentary democracy refers to democratic systems that place popular sovereignty in an elected assembly, while *presidential* democracy is a system that puts most power in the hands of an elected chief executive.

Aleatory democracy, where power is distributed by lottery, was quite popular in ancient Athens, and is still present in many modern democracies in the method used to select jurors for court trials.

Participatory democracy is more a definition of hope than reality, but describes systems where the whole populace takes an active role in government, much as was the Athenian, ancient ideal.

Monitory democracy is a term coined to describe the prevalence of non-governmental organizations and watchdogs in today's democracies trying to keep elected governments on the straight and narrow.

Banyan democracy describes the intricate complexities and contradictions within India's democratic system, which more generally might come under the heading of *pluralist* democracy, democratic systems created to manage apparently self-contradicting diversity of many kinds.

▲ The triumph of secular democracy: Eleanor Roosevelt negotiating the Universal Declaration of Human Rights in 1948

Other qualifiers of democracy are less formal and much more substantive, involving a hybridity between one system of values and the democratic system. Often the argument is that this other value system is inherently compatible with, even the source of, the democratic system. Hence 'Christian democracy' remains a very popular concept among many Europeans, especially among traditional conservatives, because it seeks to derive the logic of modern democratic values from within the Christian tradition. 'Islamic democracy' would do the same from within Islam, as would 'Jewish democracy' from Judaism. Backers of 'secular democracy', on the other hand, regard all such derivation of democratic values from religious tradition as highly suspect, and prefer to regard 'democracy' as the product of either areligious principles or as a response to the problems caused to human political relations by religious oppression and strife.

▶ Market and liberal democracy

A couple of terms are worthy of especial note when discussing what we really mean by democracy today: 'market democracy' and 'liberal democracy'. Market democracy involves the creation and maintenance of a free market in a polity where the people rule. As such, it involves a contradiction, because the rules and commands of the market, free and fair though the market might be (in principle at least) and involving the same set of people as the constituents of 'the people', are nevertheless always liable to conflict with the popular will as expressed in its political, not economic, form. There is a fundamental difference of perspective between the marketplace and the place of political assembly, even if, in ancient Athens, those places, agora and Pnyx, were near neighbours. At the same time, the market has always been the creation of the polis, its rules determined by the people who set it up, the same people who, in a democracy, rule; therefore, there is a fundamental identity between the interests of market and polis – even when they conflict.

Much the same can be said about liberal democracy, although the intimate connection between the liberal and democratic principles is even more fundamental to our modern democracies than that between market and polis, hard though that might be to accept. There is, admittedly, a good argument to be made, much as Karl Marx suggested, that the market (capitalist) principle is inherently connected to the dialectic between liberalism and democracy. Had the market not been the basis on which the rational actor of Western economic theory *and* political theory arose – someone who was outside of the hierarchical structures of traditional society and economy, and who also required freedom from those hierarchical, restricting structures – then neither the idea of the free, rational individual (liberalism), nor the idea of the inherent equality of societal actors (democracy) would have won through. 'Liberal democracy' is from this perspective a product of the triumph of the market principle of capitalism.

Even though the connection between market democracy and liberal democracy is therefore a strong one, what is special about 'liberal democracy' is that it is the powerful combination of two conflicting *political* principles, and in this relationship the liberal principle was prior. Liberal democracy is the combination of liberal governmental form with democratic content: the idea of keeping government limited and controlled, while extending the group maintaining that control to include the whole of the populace. That is why large parts of what we now regard as 'democracy' are designed to restrict the power of government over individuals, and indeed to take power away from tyrants, even when the tyranny involved is the 'tyranny of the majority'. Historically, the liberal principle was prior to the democratic as well. We shall see this in greater depth later, but both in Britain and in the United

States, the idea of freedom from tyranny, the idea of the rights of the individual to his or her liberties in the face of the state, and the guarantee of these freedoms and rights by a representative body controlling the power of government, were established long before there was anything approaching democratic equality in either political system, as we now understand it. That came later, as a completion of an already present system. The French example is a little less clear cut, given the confusions of the events after 1789, but the end result was similar.

What we now call democracy is a compromise between liberal 'freedom' and democratic 'equality' in the management and control of power in a polity. Much has been made of the conflict between these two principles, indeed much of modern political thought is based on this divide, but it is just as well to point out that freedom and equality are also codependent. Free people in a democracy can only be in an equal relationship with each other and still all be free. To use historical examples: a society in which one part is unfree because it is enslaved can never be equal; and a society that enshrines inequality in orders of ranks or castes can never, by definition, be one in which all are free. For all to be free, therefore, they must also all be equal – if in no other way, equally free. Neither freedom nor equality can ever be the universal principle of a society without the other – democracy lies in the field of tension between the two.

The problem is how to maintain that tension without one or other of the principles overcoming the other and the creative tension between the two thus being lost. If personal freedom results in some having more political or social power than others, or in some having more economic power (money and capital) than others in the free marketplace, then the political or economic inequality that results might also endanger the rights and power of those on the losing end of the equation. This is the danger to modern democracy of oligarchy (the rule of the few) and plutocracy (the rule of money). If a society wishes to counter the trends to inequality inherent in the market and in social and political circumstance by using its collective power to enforce either equality of status and condition, or equality of opportunity, then this has the clear potential of infringing and unduly limiting personal freedom. Democracy can be democracy's worst enemy.

Fortunately, the potential extremes in both of these tendencies can be avoided by the art of what Bernard Crick rightly defined as the proper form of 'politics' – the practice of finding agreement and compromise between competing and different interests within the polis in the pursuit of the common good. Current trends suggest that social and economic developments on the national and global levels will need the 'liberal democracy' that we now live by on a largely national level to transform into something closer to a 'social democracy' on the one hand and a 'pluralist democracy' on the other, combined. The contention of this book is that we should – with the use of politics properly understood – be able to accomplish this further transformation and synthesis for the good of all, for 'democracy' remains our best hope of achieving that common good.

3

Where did democracy come from? Forms of government

'If we start with the classic story of democracy, as the story of government by the people, what is remarkable is how fragile, discontinuous, even deceptive, this story is.'

ALL THAT MATTERS

The conventional origin of democracy is in ancient Greece, specifically Athens in 507 BCE with the introduction of the new constitution written by Cleisthenes. This has been a very persuasive starting point, for two reasons. First, the Western democratic tradition sees itself as being rooted in ancient Greece – even the English word for government by the people is based on a Greek root: *demos* (people) plus *kratia* (rule). Second, alternative origins, such as the *things* of ancient and early medieval northern Europe and the *ganas* and *sanghas* of sixth-century-BCE India, are rather obscure and unconvincing. Yet it could just as well be said that arguing about *the* origin of modern democracy is beside the point.

If democracy as we know it is a hybrid, as I claim in Chapter 2, then there can have been no *one* origin of democracy. Instead, its various contributing factors each have their own origin and narrative; most, not all, derive from the European experience, but that is mainly because modern democracy is largely a Western product – regardless of how universal a solution for the problems of human political organization. Modern democracy is about government by the people, but it is also about freedom from government. Furthermore, it is about 'governing ourselves', self-government, as well as representative government. Representative democracy is itself a hybrid term, because representative government is not necessarily democratic – it depends on who is being represented, who is included as being of the people. Our democracies, which include almost all of the adult population as full, voting citizens, are a rather new phenomenon, even in the West.

There are therefore at least four main components to our democracy: personal liberty; self-government; representative government; finally, the equal inclusion of all of the populace in the process of governance. One could add the rule of law as a necessary condition for these four, and the economic freedom of the market could also merit its own place. Modern democracy is also pluralist: it is accepting of diversity within the polis; yet it also now includes the principle of community and social solidarity. The point is that the development of each of these (now eight!) factors has its own narrative, and none of them can stand on its own in explaining modern democracy, but rather all need to be combined together to see the full picture of where democracy comes from.

▶ A fragile history

If we start with the classic story of democracy, as the story of government by the people, what is remarkable is how fragile, discontinuous, even deceptive, this story is. First, it is clear that Athenian democracy was not very democratic in some central respects. The *demos* on which democracy was based was far narrower than our democratic franchise. Only free male Athenians over 20 years of age could take part in ruling the polis (politics). Moreover, the leisure time of those male citizens on which democracy depended was made possible by employing resident aliens (without citizenship) as servants or by the ubiquitous use of slaves. This was nothing like a universal suffrage even for the male population, once alien servants and slaves were reckoned in. Overall, only about 20 per cent of the populace could vote.

The Athenian system was very sophisticated and its example is fundamental and inspiring to our current democratic tradition, for instance Pericles' idea of the way in which democracy combined freedom and equality. It practised the concept of being judged by your peers (in juries chosen by lottery), and it had interesting conflict-mitigating institutions such as ostracism. But it was far from perfect: being judged by one's peers did not protect one from what we would regard as undue punishment, such as the execution of Socrates in 399 BCE. Plato, Socrates' pupil, was notoriously hostile to his native city's democracy, because of its pandering to the ignorant mob. Aristotle also was sceptical about democracy, preferring the 'mixed constitution' Lycurgus wrote for Sparta, which involved monarchic, aristocratic and democratic elements. This was nearer the ideal of balance for Aristotle than the constitution of Athens.

Once Athens lost its independence, coming under first Macedonian and then Roman overlordship, the scholarly consensus, largely based on Aristotelian authority, was formed that Athenian-style democracy had been inferior to other forms of government, especially Sparta's mixed constitution and the constitution of the Roman republic. It was only in the 1840s, with the rediscovery and re-evaluation of Athenian democracy by George Grote, that Athens became rehabilitated as a model to emulate. In other words, throughout the period when many of the central institutions of what we now call democracy were developed, the Athenian model was ignored or viewed as a lesson of what not to do.

▲ The birthplace of democracy?: The Pnyx was the gathering place of classical Athens' popular assemblies.

Other historical examples of rule by the people, even if only by free men, are not that common, and so it is hard to create a continuous narrative about 'rule by the people'. It can well be argued that some form of primitive democracy has often been employed by humans, from the earliest clan alliances on, but this 'democratic' approach usually took place on a small scale. When the principle rose to anything higher it tended to be subverted and overcome by other principles of rule: patriarchy, oligarchy, aristocracy, monarchy or theocracy. The Indian *gana*s suffered this fate, and the northern European examples of government by assemblies of free men, the Icelandic Alting, Viking *ting*s, and Germanic *thing*s of the early Middle Ages, were soon subsumed into much more clearly monarchic systems where the assemblies had little, if any, real power. Muslim society had some institutions that produced more egalitarian relations than Christendom's religious and social hierarchies, but political power was largely wielded by the caliphs and later the Ottoman emperors, with little popular input.

The Swiss assemblies

One area where direct democracy (of free men) did survive and flourish was in some Swiss cantons, where ancient egalitarian farming customs became reflected in similarly egalitarian political practices of vote by assembly. These institutions only survived, however, because the mountainous terrain protected the cantons from their putative feudal overlords, the Habsburgs, who campaigned to subdue them for much of the Middle Ages. Had the Habsburgs succeeded, direct democracy would not have survived in Switzerland either.

▶ Another history: the independent republic

Mention of the Swiss and the Habsburgs suggests another narrative stream: self-government. This is the story of 'freedom from tyranny' and outside rule, liberty as autonomy; it does not necessitate rule by 'the people'. A major part of the story is the founding of the Roman Republic in the violent overthrow of a tyrant. The 'republic' – literally the *res publica*, the public thing – was less democratic than the Greek systems. The constitution had popular elements, such as the elected tribunes, but it provided in the Senate for a very strong role for the wealthy and powerful, the 'few' (oligarchy) or the 'best' (aristocracy), depending on one's viewpoint.

Many subsequent republics might pride themselves on being free – of monarchic or imperial rule – but, much like Rome, they were far from being democratic. Instead, the norm was an 'aristocratic republic' in which a nobility or a patriciate held power, often in a web of complex constitutional arrangements. The two greatest republics in early modern Europe were the Venetian and Dutch republics, both independent mercantile powers, both champions of freedom, as they saw it, but both aristocratic in their constitutions, reserving power to relatively few. The aristocratic or patrician nature of the city-states in the Hanseatic League in northern Europe or in medieval and Renaissance Italy was similar. Italian theorists such as Marsiglio of Padua might base the cities' liberty on the sovereignty of the people (as opposed to emperor or pope), but 'the people' hardly ever comprised more than a small part of the male populace.

This experience of self-government did create, however, a great heritage of constitutional systems, and a sense of the value of 'liberty', both for individual citizens and for the state itself. European culture was especially influenced by the civic humanism that emanated from the

Italian city-states, with Niccolò Machiavelli being its most famous exponent. Yet, as the latter's *The Prince* (1532) suggests, republican self-government usually ended up in some form of monarchy: Rome became an empire; Machiavelli's Florence became, effectively, the monarchy of the Medici dynasty. Many of these city-states, Florence included, were eventually absorbed by larger territorial powers, such as the Habsburgs.

▶ The development of representative democracy

The central narrative in the history of modern democracy is of the development of representative government. This is often seen as originating in England because of the significance of the English parliament. This institution was based on the Great Councils of Norman kings, but it emerged in the thirteenth century as a permanent body representing not only the nobility and Church but also the counties and towns (boroughs) – the commons. It eventually became both the main vehicle of royal power as the forum in which the king obtained revenue and passed laws, and also the place where the monarch was obliged to consult the lords and the representatives of the commons, and to hear and act on their grievances, if they were to consent to the revenues he requested. He also was expected to respect the rights and 'liberties' of the members of parliament and those they represented in return for their obedience. This quid pro quo set the frame for the representative democracy that we mostly live under today.

It is a mistake, however, to think of this as being a uniquely English development. The first parliament where this exchange between monarch and the representatives of the nobility, clergy and townsfolk took place was the *cortes* of León in Spain in 1188. The practice of kings calling parliaments to hear grievances, gain advice and raise revenue, spread across Europe. In certain respects, representative government was older still. The idea of a king calling a council of his vassals for advice and support long preceded formal parliaments. Moreover, the feudal system might consist of a pyramidal hierarchy, but it also involved legal, contractual obligations between liege and vassal. The king was dependent for his power on his nobles, and in many cases kings were forced to make concessions of rights. The Magna Carta obtained at Runnymede in England in 1215 was far from alone in Europe in securing the rights of (noble) subjects over kings.

Elected kings

In many instances, a king literally relied on his future subjects choosing him for his position. In central and eastern Europe, for most of the Middle Ages and beyond, kingship was an elected office, albeit with the 'electorate' being a relatively small number of noblemen. The office of Holy Roman Emperor, which was supposed to be at the apex of the feudal world, was, from its start in the tenth century, always an elected one, with the election in the hands of the 'prince electors', the major secular and clerical German rulers, right down to 1806. The kings of Poland, Bohemia and Hungary were also all elected by the noble estates well into the seventeenth century, the Polish king until the late eighteenth century.

The head of Christendom, the Pope, was also elected, by the College of Cardinals, and the Church offered another source of authority and power that challenged secular royal and imperial power throughout the medieval and early modern era. Both the Church and the Empire not only undermined each other's power in a series of conflicts, but they each had complex constitutional underpinnings. The conflict between emperor and pope eventually led to the Council of Constance of 1414–18, which saw a conciliarist theory of the Church putting the community of Christians and their representatives above the Pope.

Throughout the Middle Ages kings and emperors had to deal with assemblies of 'estates'. Each estate, usually representing the nobility, clergy and townsfolk, voted separately by 'chamber', as Lords and Commons did in England. These estate assemblies were effectively parliaments, and some estates, such as the Polish nobility, obtained far more liberties in the sixteenth century than the English parliament had obtained. It can be argued that the only reason why England's parliament became the 'mother of parliaments' was that it was the only major one to survive – and then take power – in the era of royal absolutism that followed the wars of religion of the sixteenth and seventeenth centuries.

Instead of submitting to their monarch, as did most Continental estates, the English estates, as represented in parliament, executed theirs. The regicide of Charles I in 1649 shocked the civilized world, and the Commonwealth regime that followed proved only a short interregnum, However, the net effect of the English Civil War (1642–51), reconfirmed in the Glorious

Revolution of 1688, was to make parliament – and the interests represented therein – the superior power in the land, the instrument not of the monarch so much as the aristocracy, the 'political nation', that dominated the membership of *both* its houses. Influential observers, such as Voltaire and Montesquieu, came to see Britain's system of limited, constitutional monarchy, as a model of the modern state. Checks and balances between monarch and parliament appeared to assure individual freedom, and yet parliamentary power and commercial wealth enabled the financing of repeated military success (especially against absolutist France).

▶ Democratic revolutions

The success of the American Revolution of 1776–83 against this model modern state was a disaster for Britain, but yet another advance in representative government. It was the successful revolt of 13 variations on the English parliament against that parliament and its 'tyrannical' monarch, George III. The purported grounds of the revolt also spoke volumes: 'No taxation without representation.' It was because the British political system had not been representative *enough*, in its new imperial form, that it lost its American colonies. In America there now began an experiment in how to turn 13 representative governments without a monarch into a united representative *self*-government. The first answer, the Articles of Confederation, was a failure; the second, the Constitution of the United States of America of 1787, has proven a success. It replaced the hereditary monarch with an elected one (the president), at the head of a federal state full of checks and balances and guarantees, many structured on examples from the already extant record of representative and self-government, but with crucial innovations. In typically evolutionary manner, one of these, the Supreme Court, only revealed its full 'democratic' effectiveness several decades after its institution, when Chief Justice John Marshall was able to establish it as a fully co-equal, independent branch of government.

The American Revolution in turn was a major contributor to the other landmark in the evolution of modern democracy: the French Revolution of 1789. The French absolute monarchy bankrupted itself aiding the American rebellion against Britain's representative government, for the principles of representative government. When the French monarchy was forced to go to its subjects for financial help, the political nation insisted that it follow the example set by Britain and America. The French Revolution started as an attempt to introduce representative government to France.

It was far more than this, however. With the American and French Revolutions the history of democracy reaches a critical stage and gets more complex. To understand the full import of the revolutions and their aftermath for that history, we need to introduce more narratives: of the rule of law, the state, equality, individual liberty, the market and civil society.

4

Where else did democracy come from? The rule of law, the state and civil society

'The notion of government as a contract between consenting individuals under law, in which the "inalienable" rights of the individual are protected, remains central to our democracy.'

The rule of law is inherently a limit on the power of 'government by the people'. Yet it is seen as a primary component of modern democracy. Central to it is the tradition of Magna Carta and the need to have legal restraints that protect the individual rights of the people from the power of the ruler. The American and French Revolutions both, in their different ways, raised the question of what happens to the rule of law when the ruler *is* 'the people'. One standard answer in modern democracies has been to institute an independent judiciary, to prevent government abuse of citizens' rights. This is a crucial element, but it is only the result of something deeper: that both liberty and equality in modern democracy depend on the power of the state – beyond government.

The German word for 'rule of law' is *Rechtsstaat*, literally law-state. This indicates much more directly the intimate connection of the rule of law with the state. The history of the rule of law goes back into the mists of antiquity. The history of the concept of the modern state goes back to the attempts of the city-states of fourteenth-century Italy to justify their independence from emperor and pope. Two aspects of the state are central to our democracy: the idea of 'a form of public power' (as the English political scientist Quentin Skinner phrases it) that is beyond both ruler and ruled; and the uniform, direct relation of each of the members of the state to that power. The combined effect of these two factors is the democratic value of legal equality.

▶ Equality and freedom

The three monotheistic religions might uphold the principle of human equality on a spiritual level, but the political and legal reality, including in Western Christendom, was different. The complex institutions of medieval Europe might foster the principles of representative government, but they were systems of inequality and subordination: of the Church over its clergy; or the noble's manorial jurisdiction over *his* peasants. Medieval 'liberty' assumed inequality: noble liberty meant being subject to a different legal system than inferiors. The expansion of state power removed legal inequality by overcoming the corporate bodies that stood between state and subject.

Lutheranism's acceptance of the secular ruler's supremacy over the Church was a factor boosting state power (in England and elsewhere). More significant was the subsequent chaos of the religious wars of the sixteenth and seventeenth centuries which suggested that the only guarantee of order was the all-powerful state described in Thomas Hobbes's *Leviathan* (1651). The political science model of the 'Westphalian state' – a state that is exclusive sovereign over all subjects in its territory – was a product of this time. In Britain the consolidation of power led to the sovereignty of the monarch-in-parliament; elsewhere to royal absolutism, which was driven by the *'politique'* sense that the interests of the state (*raison d'état*) were paramount.

In the eighteenth century this logic led to 'enlightened absolutism', under which the ruler as 'first servant of the state' was to rule by the tenets of Reason – uniformity and utility – rather than superstition or tradition. State bureaucracy should replace indirect, feudal rule with a direct relationship between subject and state. Noble and clerical privileges were to be swept aside, the peasantry emancipated. In Austria, under Joseph II, the new legal code regarded all subjects as equal *citizens* (the *Bürgerrecht*). Estates were, for him, bastions of privilege that could be ignored, even abolished, in the interests of the state and the people. Hence his statement to the leaders of the Brabant estates on 6 June 1789: 'I do not need your consent for doing good.' He abolished them a few weeks later. At the same time in Versailles, the Abbé Sieyès was proposing doing away with the privileged aristocratic and clerical estates, in favour of the common, Third Estate, in the interests of equality and the state.

Joseph II thought that the French just wanted to do what he was already doing – and in removing privilege and promoting equality he was partially correct. Yet Joseph II proved mistaken in dismissing the need for consent – not from the estates perhaps, but from the governed. The narrative of the law-state within democracy's story is not only about equality, but also liberty – the individual's rights in relation to ruler and state, and the need for consent.

As with equality, the religious concept of spiritual freedom did not necessarily translate into universal political or legal freedom, as the long history of serfdom and also slavery in Europe attests. Subordination in pyramidal hierarchies, not freedom, was the norm. The idea of the natural rights of the human being, however, survived from ancient philosophy and developed as part of the natural law theory of Thomas Aquinas from the thirteenth century on. The revolution in religious authority that culminated in the Reformation also revolutionized understanding of political authority. Concepts of religious freedom merged with secular concepts of liberty, developed by Renaissance civic humanism, and ancient traditions of Roman law, to justify the right of resistance of the 'godly individual' to an 'ungodly tyrant'. In Scotland the covenanters' movement culminated in the National Covenant of 1638, which was open to all godly individuals to sign, regardless of status or even gender. It made obedience to the ruler a matter of consent, conditional on the ruler following the covenant.

The structure of the covenant proved applicable to secular concerns. The *Agreement of the Free People of England* published by the radical Levellers in 1649 pointed this way. Some decades later, John Locke formulated the idea of government as a legally binding 'social contract' between free individuals, who retain the right to withdraw their consent if their legal rights are abused. The actual government of Britain in the eighteenth century was an aristocracy-dominated alliance between monarch and parliament, with personal rights secured by English law, but its theoretical legitimacy became that of a (fictional) social contract between all free individuals in the polity, who pooled their natural rights in 'civil society' by mutual consent for mutual benefit.

▶ The age of revolution

A key American complaint in 1776 was that this contract – and their rights as Englishmen – had been breached, but in English law there was nothing restraining the power of the monarch-in-parliament. American colonists, unrepresented in parliament, had no legal recourse against parliament's sovereign decisions. There was no remedy beyond government – except withdrawing consent. The Declaration of Independence of 1776 appealed to the inalienable rights that had been ostensibly denied. After their successful revolution, the Americans' eventual remedy against this 'tyranny' was to provide in the *written* Constitution for an independent Supreme Court to protect legal rights from the two other branches of the government: legislative and executive. A Bill of Rights was appended to the Constitution in 1791 explicitly to secure them. Protection of personal liberty by due process was built into the American *state.*

The French Revolution proclaimed the Declaration of the Rights of Man and of the Citizen in 1789. Yet this was not as effective as its American counterpart in securing rights under the rule of law, and the revolution became more a case study in the problems in establishing democracy than an inspiration for it (although it has remained that, too). The Terror confirmed for many the predictions of Edmund Burke that the revolution was simply too radical a solution to France's problems. Combining equality with liberty in a constitutional, representative government when the society was not used to either was always going to be difficult. It became nigh impossible with economic crisis and constant warfare against the forces of 'reaction' after 1792. The French experiment in Jacobin democracy (the Convention of 1792 was elected by universal male suffrage) was soon enough replaced by a much less egalitarian regime, and then by Napoleon Bonaparte's empire. This was effectively a version of enlightened absolutism. One of its greatest and characteristic achievements was rationalizing the legal system in the Napoleonic Code – the French rule of law.

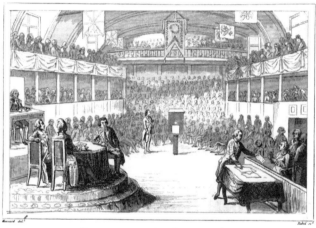

Interrogatoire de Louis le dernier

▲ The trial of Louis XVI by the French Republic's National Convention in 1792

The democratic moment of the French Revolution had long passed before Napoleon's final defeat in 1815 by the forces of 'order'. Meanwhile, however, the early nineteenth century saw modern democracy's advance in the Americas. While the new Latin American republics soon ran into difficulties, the North American experiment of the United States of America, with universal *white* male suffrage established by the 1820s, became something of a model case for 'democracy'. The liberal French aristocrat Alexis de Tocqueville was certainly convinced on his travels in the new American republic that this was the future of modern politics, in Europe as well as America. In his *Democracy in America* (published in two volumes, the first in 1835 and the second in 1840) – still seen by many as the classic explication of the American forms of democracy for its sympathetic, insightful and, at times, very critical portrayal of the developing society and polis – Tocqueville described the forms of representative self-government at the federal and state levels; the direct democracy evident at the local level (based on his experience of New England townships); and the legal – and, to a large extent, social – equality of American citizens, as well as their great sense of personal freedom. Tocqueville also described other aspects that were now becoming part of the democratic acquis, both in America and by mid-century in Europe, too. These had to do with how individuals related to each other within a democratic, non-hierarchical polity: the market and civil society.

▶ Democracy and the free market

The market was a crucial aspect of democratic America. The concept of the individual as a rational actor in the marketplace received its classic elaboration in Adam Smith's *The Wealth of Nations* (1776). Smith's work was an economic version of the social contract: the secret of prosperity was that much more wealth was produced by the division of labour and the exchange of products in the marketplace than could ever be achieved through individuals providing for themselves alone. Far from lauding individual self-sufficiency, Smith demonstrated that wealth was due to the complete mutual interdependence of all through the market. He sought to create a level playing field for market participants, and the abolition of all restraints and privileges that, ironically, merchants and manufacturers had carved out for themselves. Smith's approach was eminently democratic: it sought equality (of status) and freedom for rational actors in an economy that operated best when free of artificial restraints. Yet the economy still depended on the enforcement of contract by the state.

This laissez-faire approach of the 'free market' suited the economic expansion of America, which was without the European hierarchies or restraints on economic resources. In Europe there were many more obstacles to a free market, but the success of the relatively free British economy in leading the Industrial Revolution led to great prestige for 'liberal' economic ideas, and for the new producers of this wealth, the new middle classes. It was to accommodate them that the first real breakthrough in the 'democratization' of English politics took place with the Reform Bill of 1832. This rationalized the franchise on the basis of those with 'legitimate' interests in how government was run. One of the most powerful results was the Smithian repeal of the Corn Laws in 1846, a large blow to landed, aristocratic privilege. The 1832 electoral reform expanded the franchise only modestly, but it paved the way for future expansions. The leading contemporary British political philosophy, Utilitarianism, came to justify universal manhood suffrage – where all adult men (usually those over 21) had the vote in electing the government – as the only way in which 'the greatest number' could protect their (primarily economic) interests. The initial push for expansion of the franchise, it should be noted, was normally very gender specific. Political philosophers who accepted gender equality (such as John Stuart Mill) were rare. It took a long time even for 'democrats' to accept that women might also have their own interests to protect as rational actors.

Tocqueville also saw American democracy as a new model of social formation. Without European hierarchies and corporate bodies, Americans created a panoply of free associations in the economy, cultural life, religion, and politics. Tocqueville saw these associations of free individuals as substituting for aristocracies as 'intermediary powers' in society. They can also be seen as creating a civil society – as an association of associations, almost independent of the state – in which horizontal, egalitarian relations outweighed vertical hierarchical structures. In Tocqueville's aristocratic foil for American democracy, England, vertical relations of deference were also giving way to the same sort of associational life he described in America, especially among the new middle classes. In continental Europe as well associational life took hold: even in central Europe in the first half of the nineteenth century, where *political* association was largely prohibited, cultural and social associational life flourished, and its practices – holding meetings, speaking, and voting – prepared its participants for representative politics.

▶ The development of liberal democracy

By mid-century the logic of modern democracy began to take hold in Europe – and find greater reality in America. Tocqueville's 'democracy' in America, as he made clear, rested on the oppression by the white settlers of Native Americans and black slaves. It took the Civil War, defeat of the Confederacy, the abolition of slavery and the instituting of universal manhood suffrage in 1870, regardless of race, to erase some of the blatant exclusions of American 'democracy', although the subsequent failure to protect African American rights in the South undid much of this progress.

In Europe the promise of the 'springtime of the peoples' in 1848 for constitutional government and democratic rights proved vain with the revolutions' defeat. Yet economic and social change, the intellectual prestige of liberal ideology, the growth of an educated and propertied middle class, and the exigencies of financial crisis did eventually produce more or less constitutional, partially representative governments through much of western and central Europe. Much of this had to do with the new economic elites' demands for some say in government. In Austria, Anselm Rothschild was reputed to have told Emperor Franz Joseph in 1860: 'No constitution, no money.' Walter Bagehot's interpretation of the role of the Cabinet in the *English Constitution* (1867) made it appear as though Britain was being run by a company board for its shareholders.

This was more a liberal than a democratic world: a civil society of free associations and a free press for the propertied and educated – not yet for the 'lower classes'. The Chartist movement's demand for universal manhood suffrage in the 1840s was rejected by the now ruling middle classes. Liberal theorists such as Walter Bagehot and John Stuart Mill decried the threat of the numerically overwhelming working classes imposing their selfish interests on the body politic. Mill, in principle, would have given qualified women the vote, as he would qualified men, but there were so few qualified of either sex (owing to illiteracy, lack of a fiscal interest, reliance on public alms, and other disqualifiers) that the net effect was that 'universal suffrage' would have been given to very few. He so feared the 'tyranny of the majority' that he wanted to restrict governmental interference with the individual as much as possible. Mill's *On Liberty* (1859) remains one of the most influential reasons why modern democracy is so liberal – in its intent to restrict popular power over the individual.

The extension of suffrage

Despite liberal doubts, the vote was eventually expanded. In Britain, the expansion of the franchise to include most of the lower classes occurred in 1867 (for towns) and 1884 (for counties). Even then only about 60 per cent of men, and no women, had the vote. In France, after various false starts, universal manhood suffrage was established in 1875 (French women did not get the vote until 1944). Switzerland had universal manhood suffrage from 1848; Italy from 1913; some Scandinavian countries, Finland and Norway, had universal suffrage by 1914, but the franchise was still restricted in most of Europe at that time. Interestingly enough, universal suffrage enjoyed more progress in the British settler colonies, especially New Zealand and Australia. There was universal manhood suffrage in the former in 1879, and universal suffrage including women in 1893. Australia followed, for federal elections, in 1902.

In central Europe, the German Empire had universal manhood suffrage at the imperial level from 1871, but it retained strongly anti-democratic features, and various restricted and divided (curial) franchises at the more important level of the constituent states. Austria enacted universal manhood suffrage for elections to the Austrian parliament in 1907, partly as a result of a campaign by Austrian socialists. The other half of the Dual Monarchy, Hungary, retained a restricted franchise aimed at preserving Magyar national (and gentry) domination of the multinational kingdom.

If democracy had made significant headway by the early twentieth century, it still had to come to terms with two aspects that became only partial and controversial aspects of modern democracy: socialism and nationalism, or, more neutrally, community and diversity.

5

Where has democracy got to lately? Community and diversity

'Nationalism is usually democracy's wicked uncle.'

ALL THAT MATTERS

In Europe in 1914 only France, Italy and a few western and northern European states could claim to be democracies; Britain only had partial manhood suffrage, lagging behind her own colonies. American democracy was compromised by racially segregating Jim Crow laws, which effectively excluded African Americans in the South from their democratic and civil rights until at least the 1960s. The other major powers either had only partly constitutional, partly democratic government (Germany and Austria-Hungary) or something much worse (Russia). Much of the rest of the world was under the control of European empires, in which only settler colonies had anything approaching democratic institutions. Today democracy is much more established, and can claim to be the predominant governmental form in the world. Its path to such prominence has not been straightforward – anything but. Democracy had to confront other powerful ideological challengers for the authority of 'the people' – socialism and nationalism – and then their extreme successors – communism and fascism. For long stretches it looked as though democracy would lose out.

Two new narratives need to be introduced at this point: community and diversity. Both can be positive aspects, vital aspects indeed, of modern democracy. Community as solidarity or 'fraternity', the sense of shared interests and values, of a moral connection with other citizens, is what keeps democracies together. Diversity, as the recognition and respect for difference, is vital for allowing co-operation in those areas where we do share the same interests. The problems with both aspects arise when they get out of hand and take over from democracy.

▶ Community

The concept of community, especially religious community, has an ancient lineage, and there are many historical examples of attempts to establish godly communities, including the 'New Zion' of the Anabaptists of Münster and – less notoriously – the Puritan colonies of New England. Religiously informed concepts of community, such as the Earl of Shaftesbury's Evangelicalism, continued to provide critiques of the modern economy and civil society. The most relevant form of community for democracy, however, was socialism. The modern socialist movement was a response to the consequences of the increase of inequalities and distress, and the perceived injustices, of the new, industrial, free-market economy. Adam Smith's model of market self-regulation and mutual benefit for all individual participants did not quite work out as well, or at least as equitably, in reality. Civil society under liberal leadership was not effective enough in relieving resulting poverty and squalor.

Advocates for the lower classes demanded universal manhood suffrage, and workers formed associations (unions) to further their interests by themselves. Initially, these efforts were resisted even in liberal Britain, but British socialists largely operated within the rules of British politics, thinking their programme of social justice could be achieved within the system. Fears among the propertied were still strong that the working-class vote would, effectively, be a 'licence to pick pockets', and there was a genuine question as to how far the socialist programme infringed on the individual's 'right' to property. However, the rule of law and individual liberty also meant respecting the right of the newly enfranchised working class to their representatives. By 1914 the Labour Party had become the third force in mainland British politics.

There was never a simple conflict between socialism and the market economy. On the European continent especially, there were always pre-existing privileged classes, pre-existing religious establishments, and there was also a stronger tradition of direct state intervention on behalf of the lower classes. Social welfare programmes that cut across laissez-faire economic policies were adopted much more strongly in countries such as Germany and Austria than in Britain. At the same time, the relative lack of a liberal tradition of political freedom meant that socialism was actively suppressed – by the state. Conversely, the dominant Continental version of socialism was based on Karl Marx's analysis of capitalism, which saw the only remedy to the proletariat's oppression as a revolution that would entirely overturn not only the government but also the state, and all its bourgeois rights to property and the like. Socialist practice on the Continent was normally pragmatic and law-abiding as in Britain: the socialists officially called themselves Social Democrats. Yet socialist theory (and rhetoric) was more revolutionary, and to that extent against what we now see as modern democracy. Replacing the Third Estate with the working class as the universal 'people' was one thing, but replacing civil society with a dictatorship of the proletariat was not 'democratic'.

▶ Diversity

Diversity is an even more amorphous term than community – but it is still vital to modern democracy. In its most positive form, it is the liberal pluralism that allows for religious, cultural, ideological, ethnic and social differences, to name a few. It is the virtuous equilibrium caused by James Madison's conflict and competition between interests and factions; the culture clash of Karl Popper's open society; or the differences of opinions and interests that are the grist to the mill of Isaiah Berlin's conflict-management model of liberal democracy. Were democracy not to have a place for diversity, Indian democracy would be quite impossible. Yet it used to be that difference was frowned on when it came to democratic politics, because, as the adage goes: what differentiates, also divides. Accepting diversity, therefore, was seen as inviting division, and breaking up the democratic consensus. In many ways, this has indeed happened, too often in recent history in too many parts of the world, because there were differences, diversities, that proved stronger than the bonds of democracy's civil society.

There are aspects of diversity that do not sit well with democracy. Friedrich Nietzsche's suggestion, for instance, that the strong, the beautiful and the powerful should be freed from the shackles of the 'slave morality' of equal rights is clearly anti-democratic. Social Darwinism's biologistic claim that progress lay in embracing the inequalities of the free-market economy, and not having the state intervene in the 'natural' 'struggle for existence', also strained the basic democratic appeal to human equality and popular self-government. Discrimination (recognition of difference) on racial and gender lines might have been accepted historically, but it also contravened democratic logic. If democracy benefitted from the state's drive for rational uniformity against particularism and legal differentiation, it also suffered when that uniformity was challenged by ideologies recognizing particularist differences, whether ancient or modern.

The greatest challenge of diversity to democracy was, and remains, nationalism. This might seem odd, as the nation has often been seen as the basic unit of democracy, the totality in which democracy happens. How can 'government by the people' not be national, when 'the people' is the nation? Yet nationalism is about diversity, difference, not unity. Some of the confusion arises in the fact that 'nation' and 'state' are often thought of as the same. The United Nations, for instance, would be better called the United States, were that name not already taken. Some versions of nationalism, such as 'civic nationalism', are also, in theory, completely compatible with modern democracy, because all citizens, regardless of other identities, are members of the nation/state. But this is not how most nationalism works. Nationalism is usually democracy's wicked uncle.

▶ The challenge of nationalism

Historically, nation and state were allied – both were particularist reactions to claims of universal authority and power (empire and papacy). Ideologically, however, national*ism* was a reaction to the universalist concept of the individual rational actor – it cut across and dissolved this concept of a uniform, rational humanity. Building on Romanticism's embrace of originality, nationalism stressed the inadequacies of the 'rational actor' (see Chapter 2) to describe the multiplicity of human societies. Johann Gottfried Herder's emphasis on human diversity (now seen as multiculturalist) gave a theoretical foundation to nationalism, by which the 'natural' form of government is by a human community's own kind, in their own customary manner, in their own nation, a *partial* totality among many. The nation could be defined in many ways, from language, to historical fate, birth right and 'race', but belonging to the nation was a different relationship to being a citizen of the state. It was especially so when national belonging became, increasingly, a matter of 'blood', membership of a distinct ethnic group: ethnonationalism.

Nationalism's goal has been to enable all nations to have their own nation-state, but this is easier said than done. In some cases, this created movements of national unification, as in Germany and Italy in the mid-nineteenth century, but it has also encouraged the division of multiethnic states, such as the Habsburg Monarchy, along ethnic lines, even when there were not so much ethnic lines as splotches. Nationalism usually ignored the lessons of its origins, because, once the previously 'oppressed' ethnonational minority gained power in its 'nation-state', it invariably then began denying the right of other ethnonational minorities within its borders to be different. Nationalists might claim that 'we just want to be free', but this always seemed to clash with the rights of members of other minorities within the same nation-state to be free, too. Nationalist movements in Europe were almost all hives of anti-Semitism, because a diasporic minority such as the Jews simply did not fit the nationalist model (whereas it did fit the democratic, citizen-state).

The happy co-operation of nation-states envisaged by liberal nationalists such as Giuseppe Mazzini was impossible in the context of nineteenth-century Europe, because no one could agree on what level national differentiation should stop. Instead, the concatenation of national conflicts, of nation-states looking to 'free' co-nationals in other states (irredentism), and of 'national' empires seeking a place in the sun that would Darwinistically block out the light for others – all exacerbated by social and political pressures on political elites from below – led to the upheaval of the First World War.

That war had immensely destructive consequences: it unhinged imperial forms of government in central and eastern Europe, but it did not, as promised, make the world safe for democracy. The interwar era did see, it is true, the establishment of universal suffrage, including women, in the main 'democracies' (Britain, America, not France) and in most of central Europe. Germany gained a model, democratic constitution as did many other new democracies, set up on a supposed basis of national self-determination on territories of the former empires. Socialist parties gained a large share of power, and passed progressive laws that furthered economic and social justice. Yet the overarching reality was one of trauma and continued crisis, which meant the new normalcy was always fragile.

▶ Democracy in crisis and in recovery

Most of the lands of the former Russian Empire were in perpetual crisis under Bolshevik, communist rule, an extreme perversion of socialism that put the goals of the 'community' beyond all democratic constraints. In Italy, Mussolini's fascists similarly rejected the rules of liberal democracy in favour of a radical nationalist agenda. Democratic values fared poorly in most of the rest of eastern and central Europe, too.

It was in 1928 (before the Wall Street Crash of 1929) that the Western economy began its collapse into the Great Slump. In 1933 the nemesis of liberal democracy, Hitler's National Socialist Party, having won a democratic election, was legally installed as Germany's government. Authoritarianism and nationalism were now surpassed by modern, 'scientific', racial nationalism, while socialism was challenged by communism. At the start of the Second

World War, Poland folded before the Nazi–Soviet Pact (signed on 28 August 1939) and then Germany rolled over the forces of the democracies of Britain and France in the summer of 1940. Democracy's days looked numbered.

Yet the democracies, and democracy, eventually won out. In the United States, Franklin Delano Roosevelt, under the New Deal, was able to use quasi-socialist methods to stabilize the American economy and society, in the interests of social peace – and capitalism. Britain was similarly able to reach a social and economic compromise that righted its domestic situation, and when confronted with Nazism's huge military successes in 1940 was able to call upon a nationalism that evoked both *particularist* British values and *universal* values of freedom and democracy – while being ruled in effect by a charismatic dictator (in the best sense), Winston Churchill. While it was the German attack on the Soviet Union and then the Japanese attack on Pearl Harbor that changed the dynamics of war, the net result was to vindicate the Western democracies, confirm the doggedness of the British, and reveal the immense economic and military power of the United States.

It was in the aftermath of the Second World War that the framework of today's global system was established, under an American aegis. The international system is in its core values a liberal democratic one. Fascism and National Socialism were militarily vanquished and, with their record of tyranny and genocide, morally bankrupt. Americans were able to impose on the international community a system of quasi-representative global government, the United Nations, a liberal economic system, and a system of international law based on the Universal Declaration of Human Rights of 1948. American anti-imperialism was also instrumental in forcing the European powers to give up their overseas empires, Britain's chief among them. India and Pakistan gained independence in 1947, India becoming and *remaining* the world's largest, and most complex, democracy. In the following decades Britain withdrew from most of her other imperial possessions.

There were major flaws to the new, democratic world order. By far the largest was that a crucial wartime ally had been the Soviet Union, which proceeded to take over the 'buffer zone' of the eastern half of Europe as its sphere of interest, with imposed communist governments of 'people's republics' to match. The communist takeover of China in 1949 and further attempts to expand communist influence in Greece and elsewhere led to the setting in of concrete blocks (and the Iron Curtain's barbed wire) of the Cold War – a seemingly endless stand-off between the 'Western democracies' and the 'communist bloc'.

The Cold War undermined actual democracy at home and abroad. Fears of communism led to McCarthyism in the United States and the intimidation and ostracism of many on the radical Left in other Western countries. The international deadlock between East and West allowed many anti-democratic regimes to flourish under Western protection because they were anti-communist, even when in their integral nationalist, authoritarian or, in the case of South African apartheid, racist policies they were deeply anti-democratic. Then again, much of the United States, especially the Deep South, followed racist policies such as

▲ Martin Luther King during the 'Great March on Washington' in 1963. During the 1960s the parameters of Western democracy were challenged and expanded.

segregation and voter suppression into the 1960s. In the process of decolonization, whereby imperial possessions, especially in Africa and Asia, gained independence from the Western colonial empires, the outcome was rarely a durable democracy. The choice was usually between communist takeover, or a military or nationalist (usually both) dictatorship. Even in Europe, Spain and Portugal, and Greece for a time, were run by nationalist authoritarian regimes well into the 1970s.

There were also positive trends, especially regarding diversity and community. The Civil Rights campaign in America in the 1950s and 1960s brought real democratization and liberalization, which was echoed in Europe. Pluralism, the respect for and inclusion of diverse religious, ethnic, gender and racial minorities, now became more central to democracy. There was also much progress in achieving social justice under democratic political rules, especially regarding healthcare. Nationalism was reined back, the absolute need for national sovereignty rethought. What is now known as the European Union is the greatest experiment yet undertaken in democratic, *supranational* institution building. The vast increase in prosperity in the West, and communism's failure to compete economically, led to the end of the Cold War in 1989. Since then the hybrid of modern representative, liberal, market democracy has spread into Eastern Europe (usually as part of the *acquis* of the European Union), has gained more reality and permanence in most of South America, and also been realized in large parts of Asia, including Indonesia, and Africa, including Ghana, Nigeria, and formerly apartheid South Africa.

▶ A work in progress

Large parts of the world are still not democratic. Even in the older democracies, the recent economic and financial crises have shown up large systemic flaws, with many calling for a rethinking of the social contract between capitalism and community. Nationalism has also reasserted itself, threatening the progress toward greater international collaboration both on the global level of the United Nations and at the regional level of the European Union. The American Right's paranoia concerning accepting any international treaty under the aegis of the United Nations on the grounds that it will amount to a lessening of sovereignty has often handicapped American co-operation with what is, after all, largely an American creation. This continues even under the Obama administration, due to Republican control of the House, as the fiasco of American non-funding of UNESCO illustrates. There is also the post-Cold War survival of Russian ambitions to be a top nation, as demonstrated by its vetoing of action by the international community over Syria. In Europe, the national pettiness of the response to the financial crisis, especially from Germany, has hardened hearts and minds to further integration. This is before we contemplate the potential disaster, especially for Britain, that British withdrawal from the European Union represents.

Yet there are also positive trends. The rapid growth of non-governmental organizations (NGOs) and the virtual community of the Internet have produced a 'monitory democracy' where civil society counters these negative trends. The demand in the developing world, with its burgeoning economic middle classes and civil societies, is for more democracy, not less. As the Arab Spring shows, democracy remains a work in progress, of the 'two steps forward, one step back' kind – but it *has* progressed.

Having seen what it is made of, how it was put together, and where it has got to, let us see how it works.

6

How does democracy work?

'Politics in practice can appear less than wholesome, and its results are almost always less than ideal – but then watching sausages being made is also inadvisable, no matter how delicious or nutritious the sausage.'

THAT MATTERS

Modern democracy is the product of experience. It has a long history, with many false starts, and many lessons learned, we hope. Democracy, as we know it, is a hybrid that coalesced after many centuries and is still adapting to current human realities. There is, therefore, no simple, sufficient theory of how democracy works, or ought to work. The closest we can get to a theory of our modern democracy is an abstraction from modern democratic practice.

Even when we derive a workable theory of democracy, theory and practice can often clash. We understand that what works in theory does not necessarily work in practice, but with democracy the reverse is almost as common: what works in practice does not work in theory. For instance, many of the most successful democracies today are formally hereditary monarchies, yet democracies ought *in theory* to be republics. Disentangling how democracy ought to work in theory and how it actually works in practice is inherently difficult. That said, this chapter shows how democracy works in theory; the next will discuss how our actual democracies compare to democracy's 'best practices'.

The prime goal of modern democracy is to answer the question: How best are we to govern ourselves? There is, however, a subsidiary question, asked by Rodney King (whose beating by police officers sparked the 1992 Los Angeles Riots): 'Can we all get along?' Related to this duality is the famous distinction Isaiah Berlin made between the 'two freedoms': 'negative' and 'positive'.

The two freedoms

Positive 'freedom to' is analogous to 'governing ourselves' – it is democratic power, what we are able to do together to shape our world. Negative 'freedom from' is the space in which individuals are free from government's power. It is what many past liberals sought – to get the government off our backs, to act merely as an umpire between citizens. This is now the libertarian, neoliberal or, in America – confusingly – 'conservative' position on 'democracy': that it is just a system for enabling individuals to pursue their own happiness as they see fit.

Berlin himself pointed out that negative freedom was insufficient. We need positive freedom because a major reason for having self-government is to produce the benefits that accrue to all from the synergies involved in working together. The purpose of democracy is not to gain power over others in the polity (as is the case in many other governmental systems). Democracy's purpose is, instead, to use the articulated power of all citizens together to promote the 'common good'.

Modern democracy is the best way to govern ourselves so that we can all get along *and* promote the common good.

We saw the historically derived conditions that come with modern democracy's promise of self-government. It is more a suite of items – a package deal including the following:

- government controlled by elected officials who are responsible to the electorate

- the legal right of all individuals to various freedoms, including economic freedom, free speech, association, due process and, for citizens, fair representation

- the equality of individuals under the law

- a system of social justice that secures citizens as members of the community from misfortune

- a definition of the polis's/state's specific character and membership – in other words, a law of citizenship.

Modern democracy also comes with a toolbox of institutions and procedures to achieve its goals and meet its conditions. These include: a democratic governmental structure; an electoral system; political institutions outside government; and institutions of civil society that counterbalance government.

▶ Governmental structure

There are two major forms of government in modern democracy: *parliamentary* democracy (as in Britain), and *presidential* democracy (as in the United States and France). Many parliamentary democracies are formally constitutional monarchies, where the symbolic head of state is a hereditary monarch, and the head of government – prime minister or chancellor – owes power to the fact of controlling a majority of the elected members in the main house of the legislature. Some parliamentary democracies, such as Germany, have an elected president as head of state, but the presidential office in these cases is relatively weak and largely ceremonial. In a presidential democracy, the presidency is the most powerful elected office, the president being the directly elected head of government and state. In the parliamentary system, legislative and executive power are strongly connected, but the head of state and government are separate; in the presidential system, legislative and executive power are formally divided, the head of state and government the same. Most modern democracies tend to be one of these two models, but with degrees in between.

All democracies have constitutions, usually written, sometimes, as in Britain, 'unwritten' (but with copious written commentaries). These create a complex governmental geometry of power divided between different branches of the government, and those branches relating to each other in a series of checks and balances to prevent abuse of power by any one part. Most democracies have a bicameral legislature (a parliament with an upper and lower house), often to keep the chambers mutually checked. All democracies take measures to secure the independence of the judicial branch, so that the rule of law proceeds without undue executive or legislative interference. Most democracies also make arrangements to ensure that the representatives of the people do have some control over who is on the judicial bench. The American President, for instance, nominates Supreme Court justices for life terms, and they are confirmed by the upper house of the legislature (the Senate), a procedure that, so far, has more or less worked.

An objective and ethical civil service, which governs in response to the interests of the public, rather than those of their immediate political bosses, or themselves, is also a goal of modern democracy. The watchwords of transparency and good governance figure large in discussions of democratic best practice. A bureaucracy that puts the state's interests above political pandering, but is obedient to legitimate orders from its elected leaders, is a *democratic* necessity. This is even more true when it comes to the military and security forces.

▶ Electoral systems

The form of voting in democracies is, crucially for the voter's independence, by secret ballot. It is also, or should be, 'one person, one vote': a democracy of equal citizens must ensure that each citizen has the same say in how they are governed. Voting also has to be periodic: the norm seems now to be a general election about every four years, with a maximum of five, but this varies between states. There are two basic forms of electoral system in modern democracies: *plurality* voting ('first past the post') and *proportional* representation.

In plurality voting, the winner in an election is whoever obtains the most votes, even if not a majority. This is the system used for elections in Britain and America, usually for a single office or for a single constituency seat. This can create decisive majorities for one party to govern, often based on only a minority of the vote. In Britain, the Conservative government of Margaret Thatcher (1979–1990) never obtained a majority of the vote, but still had large majorities in parliament with which to pass radical measures. A variation of this system, intended to cut down on this inadvertent result of plurality voting, is to have second-round, run-off elections between the two highest vote-getters in the first round, so that the eventual winner does have an absolute majority of the vote. This is the method currently used in France – both for presidential and legislative elections.

Proportional representation (PR) tries to apportion power according to the overarching preferences of the electorate. Some schemes apportion assembly seats (and hence power) proportionally to how the electorate voted as a whole. This is usually by party list, although countries such as Germany try to have some representatives elected by constituency, with the overall proportions made up by party list candidates. Other countries try to allow the voter to state a list of preferences, so that the vote still counts at some level even though the first choice has been defeated (single transferable vote). Voting in such schemes can get very complicated, but overall it does produce a result more reflective of the electorate's wishes. A large number of countries, including most continental European democracies – and Scotland – have some form of PR. Such systems tend to produce a multiplicity of parties and seldom produce absolute majorities for any one party. This means that the electorate hardly ever votes directly for its government, but rather votes for political parties to decide in coalition negotiations the shape of the government.

Democracy and parties

The key political institution in the toolbox of democracy is the political party. Parties were not always seen in a positive light. The American constitution has no place for them, and, as 'factions', they were initially regarded by many as unwelcome, divisive detractors from the general will. Yet soon enough it was realized that these informal institutions are crucial to democracy's success. If there were no political parties, there would, in the system of representative democracy, be no choice for the voters to make on a national level in coherent policy terms. Parties provide a vital mediation between the voter and government; they make co-ordinated political campaigns possible, and they are conduits by which grassroots opinion reaches government. Parties have been characterized as political elites competing for the electors' favour, almost as rival aristocracies. Political life as a competition between parties is nonetheless a form of democracy, if ordinary citizens can participate in that political life through well-organized, inclusive party structures, and voters' input is not overshadowed by lavish political financing by special interests.

▶ Civil society

Civil society also has vital institutions for democracy. Free media and NGOs can keep track of government and offer alternative policies. Free associations, including professional associations to lobby government, are also crucial; all sectional interests, those we like and those we do not like, need organizations to inform the people's representatives of what they think is best for them *and* the common good. A free-market economy is also a vital institution to keep economic power broadly distributed, although it needs state regulation in order to function, as well as to keep the market fair as well as free. The establishment of an independent central bank, akin to the status of the judiciary, has become another key 'democratic' institution, even though it severely reduces the power of governments to set economic policy.

Education, in most democracies, is something shared between the state and civil society. The state funds education systems and has a valid interest in setting good education policy, because it needs well-informed citizens to fulfil their role in society and the state effectively, and to exercise their political power (their vote) intelligently and responsibly. Yet education also needs to be seen as a part of civil society, independent of the state that funds it. Universities in many countries are state-funded, yet they cherish their academic freedom from political interference, because they are a major source of knowledge and social self-awareness (criticism) for the whole of society. The same can be said of state-funded cultural institutions, such as, in Britain, the BBC, which needs independence from government interference to fulfil its public (government-ordained) mission.

▶ Democracy and politics

Democracy is a complex system, and, as with any complex system, there also has to be a set of instructions. This book is only one of many books aimed at helping democracies govern themselves. The most helpful, in my opinion, are those that emphasize a pluralist approach, acknowledging society's many diversities, to achieve the common good. The way to do this in a modern democracy is through the art of politics. Bernard Crick's *In Defence of Politics* argues that democracy and politics are not the same, yet I would argue modern democracy is the most *purely* political system yet devised, because, unlike theocracy, communism, fascism or absolute monarchy, it has little, if any, blatant ideology. Its normal response to any issue is a political one: let's argue about the pros and cons, seek allies and advantage, then compromise, and then let's vote on it.

'Politics' has pejorative connotations in today's world, but politics is what makes democracy work. Crick asserts that politics properly understood is not about a struggle for power over others, but rather the art of bringing together members of the polity, their differing values and interests, and by argument, debate and, if necessary, political campaigning, eventually coming to an agreement, usually a compromise, where everyone's interests and values are pooled together to further the common good. Politics in practice can appear less than wholesome, and its results are almost always less than ideal – but then watching sausages being made is also inadvisable, no matter how delicious or nutritious the sausage. In any case, democratic politics should not be about creating perfect solutions, based on absolute decisions, one way or the other, using 'either/or' logic, but about reaching agreements where all can be accommodated, the logic of 'both/and'. Some dismiss this sort of approach as indecisive and political accommodation, but in most circumstances this is what democracy should be about – accommodation for the common good.

▶ Agreeing to disagree

A key notion in this pluralist version of democracy is W.B. Gallie's 'essentially contested concepts'. These are concepts that people disagree over, based on reasonable arguments that their opponents can acknowledge as such. Even if they do not agree with their opponents, they can respect them for their sincerity and rationality. In other words, they can agree to disagree – in political terms be a loyal opposition to the governing party, and recognized as such. Learning that it is better to 'play the game' of politics, follow the rules, and conduct electoral procedures by the book, than it is to try to crush your opponents in civil war or revolution, took modern democracies a long time. Sometimes it appears we are not there yet, but this is what democratic politics should be about: solving problems and conflicts by compromise and mutually agreed rules – politically – for the common good.

This does not mean problems go away. The concept of equality, for instance, remains hotly contested in every democracy. It is a central question of justice, but open to many interpretations. Legal equality for citizens is a given in a democracy (equal rights for non-citizens is another matter), but beyond that? Should equality of opportunity for individuals be a goal? If so, should they be born with equal opportunity, or simply have equal opportunity in the marketplace (no insider trading)? Or should equality be an equality of outcome, at least a lessening of extreme inequalities? Many who argue for the latter claim that it is necessary in order to enable equality of opportunity: How can a child born in poverty possibly have opportunities equal to a billionaire's offspring? Then again, is not equality of security enough, whereby all citizens are equal to the extent that they are secure from utter destitution (a safety net version of the welfare state)? Or 'equality of security plus', where large economic inequality is tolerable if the living standards for the poorest are higher than in any other system? All these arguments are worthy of respect, but their variance shows how far democratic respect for the views of others has to stretch.

This requires not only respect for others, but also goodwill, what Albert O. Hirschman called 'loyalty'. The source of this loyalty – what keeps the members of a democracy together through thick and thin – has historically been seen as emanating either from a sense of social community or belonging to a nation. Increasingly, however, the relatively simple structure of a unitary representative democratic system in a nation-state has been challenged by more complex, pluralist, federal and multinational systems. One of the first modern democracies, the United States, always had this sort of structure (as did Switzerland), but the emergence of the mega-democracy of India and very diverse (and large) democracies such as Indonesia, Brazil and South Africa have added more layers of democratic complexity.

The European Union, a supra-cum-multinational polity, has posed even larger questions. In such models the supposedly unitary popular sovereignty of the nation-state gives way to divided or pooled sovereignty, and questions of subsidiarity or competence become ever more complex, the power of the electorate over its rulers ever more tenuous and suspect.

The process of economic globalization nevertheless requires political change on a global scale as well. The idea of a democratic world government has been promoted for centuries, but has usually been seen as naive and impractical – impossible, even undesirable. Yet the post-1945 world is also a multilateral world of international institutions and international law. These institutions, chief among them the United Nations, are only quasi-democratic, and perforce include many non-democratic members. The question we face as a world community is whether this global system can be sufficiently democratized to make it work as well as modern democracy does. That of course assumes that modern democracy does work in practice – it is time to see how democratic our own democracies really are.

7

How democratic are our democracies?

'The public complains of not having enough influence over policy, what is called the "democratic deficit", but then fewer people bother to become members of political parties, or participate in political life.'

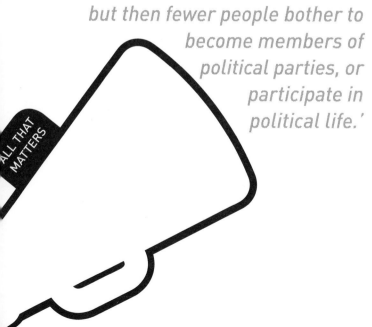

ALL THAT MATTERS

In terms of achieving their aim of maximizing the common good in such a way that all can get along, modern democracies have done remarkably well, and are getting better – despite temporary problems with the global economy. The established democracies are more prosperous and in many respects much more inclusive than they were only a few decades ago, especially in terms of minority rights and gender equality. The prospect of legalizing gay marriage would have been almost unthinkable 20 years ago. Newer democracies, chief among them India, have made massive strides of late in bringing prosperity to their peoples, even if various problems such as corruption and limits on freedom of speech persist. Then again, despite their successes, our established democracies also show deep flaws when measured even to their *own* standard of 'best practices' outlined in the last chapter.

▶ Inherent flaws

Some of our democracies' flaws are present in their very structures. In Britain, votes are not equal. This is not simply because of the different population counts of electoral districts (constituencies), which are due to redrawing of districts not keeping pace with population shifts. There are built-in asymmetries because of devolution: Scottish MPs in Westminster can vote on English matters whereas English MPs cannot vote on some Scottish matters, which are decided in Scotland's National Assembly. These are tolerable inequalities because of historical experience and political accommodation, but they are still inequalities.

Much more egregious are the inequalities in voters' power in the United States. Unlike in Britain, both houses of Congress, the American legislature, have real power. The lower house, the House of Representatives, has seats carefully allocated proportional to state population. The upper house, the Senate, which in many ways is more powerful, has two members for each state, no matter the huge disparities in populations of those states. The reason for this is that the United States began as a federal republic, not a democracy as such, and the Senate represented the pooled sovereignty of the states – it was only in 1913 that direct popular election of senators replaced election by state legislatures. The consequence in voting equality is immense: two Californian senators represent 38 million residents; two Wyoming senators represent 577,000 residents. The power of a Wyoming voter in the Senate is therefore 66 times greater than that of a Californian.

American anomalies

The electoral college through which US presidents are elected is also affected by these disproportions. That is one reason why George W. Bush became president in 2001, despite losing the popular vote to Al Gore; the other reason was the appalling organization and infrastructure of Florida's electoral system (a problem in many states, still) from butterfly ballots to hanging chads – that and the conservative majority of the US Supreme Court. It is also of note that the citizens of the American capital, Washington, DC, with a population some 632,000, more than Wyoming, have no senators and only a non-voting House member to represent them in Congress.

These inequalities are things to which Americans have become inured – they are part of the constitution. They, along with most citizenries, have also become largely accepting of other deep structural flaws in representative democracies that severely curtail the electorate's influence over government. Both of the main voting systems, plurality voting and proportional representation, tend to end up distancing government from popular input.

The British system has traditionally been seen as producing an 'elective dictatorship' – where the discipline of the party system and parliamentary sovereignty combine to produce unlimited power for the leader of the majority in the Commons, as the prime minister (there being no written constitution). Owing to plurality voting, as we saw, this immense power is usually granted to a prime minister by a minority of the voting public, and it is potentially five years before the electorate gets a chance to change its mind. If America has an elected monarch as its ruler (the president), Britain has in effect an elected monarch – the prime minister – with much greater powers, despite the presence of the hereditary monarch. This is justified as making for strong, decisive government, and comes with assurances of conventional limits on prime-ministerial power, such as the collective responsibility of the Cabinet. Yet, as elections in Britain have become more 'presidential', the prime minister's power has only increased and is even more difficult to limit.

This might change – if the dual hegemony of Labour and the Conservatives fragments in such a way that small parties are actually represented significantly in the Commons, making coalition government the norm, then this might impinge on prime-ministerial power. On the other hand, the first-past-the-post electoral system still militates against such small parties, making such a scenario unlikely; and even in the current coalition the Liberal Democrats have usually found themselves powerless to oppose the determined policy of the (Conservative) prime minister, so the presidential trend for the prime minister's power continues.

Even if a prime minister can be reined in by his Cabinet or his party (even, currently, his coalition partners), this is still only government by the few – oligarchy, at best aristocracy. What we call democratic party politics is more a competition between political elites for the electorate's favour, with the electorate more a bystander than a participant. This is particularly true in democracies with proportional representation, where a general election is in effect the first stage in an indirect election, with the second stage being the coalition-building, where parties decide among themselves which parties get to govern. This is much more a system of elected elites, of aristocracies competing with each other, than anything resembling simple democracy. The actual people do not seem to have much direct say in how they are governed. Sometimes aristocracy descends into oligarchy. For decades Austria was ruled by a 'great coalition' of ÖVP conservatives and SPÖ socialists, almost regardless of how the electorate voted. Moreover, actual power resided in the 'Parity Commission' where negotiations between the country's economic interests were then enacted by an obedient parliament. This oligarchy did an excellent job, but it was not very democratic.

Gerrymandering

Another case of oligarchy at work is what is happening on the state level in the United States. Computer mapping now allows gerrymandering of electoral districts (which in many states are decided by the state assemblies) to be so efficient that majority parties can produce situations where a minority vote will still give them a healthy majority, and only a landslide can unseat them, if then. This is a major reason why in the federal election of 2012 more Americans voted for Democrats in races for the House of Representatives, but Republicans retained a sizeable majority nevertheless. Most of the worst examples of gerrymandering at the moment come from Republicans, who, reminiscent of Jim Crow, are also at the forefront of trying to suppress the vote by making it more difficult to prove eligibility (through stricter voter ID laws) and indeed more difficult to vote (by restricting voting access in poor districts). Politicians are, in effect, choosing their electorates, rather than vice versa.

▶ The 'democratic deficit'

Part of the problem here is that voters are just not paying sufficient attention to their political systems. The public complains of not having enough influence over policy, what is called the 'democratic deficit', but then fewer people bother to become members of political parties, or participate in political life, many not even voting in general elections, let alone elections on a lower level. This means that special interests and committed groups of activists have far more influence, often a divisive one, because ordinary people do not bother to vote. Perhaps commitment to grassroots activism can be praised, but then these days the grassroots are as likely to be 'AstroTurf' as genuine – in other words, financed and organized by special interest groups from above rather than coming from below. The Tea Party phenomenon that moved so powerfully in favour of the Republicans in the 2010 off-year elections in the United States is suspiciously of this manufactured variety.

Even when the political activism is genuine, the people who are drawn to grassroots politics – on either side – tend to be more extreme and polarized in their views than the average, centre-ground voter. There have been 'radical centre' parties with mass support, but they are rare, and if one party does moderate its views (as the Democrats have under Clinton and Obama), the other party still paints their policies as extreme. Whether true or not, the result is often policies that are seen as too extreme by the moderate centre. The fact that a majority of the American public is still against 'Obamacare' – the really rather mild reform of the American healthcare system – because it is so 'extreme', points in this direction.

Then again, the argument for not voting is often that the government is not enacting the policies they promised, is not listening to the electorate, but often this is because the government is being obstructed by the opposition, which then benefits from the frustrated public not voting for the 'failed' government's representatives. Alienation of the voter, especially the less privileged voter, becomes a vicious circle.

The great divergence

The lack of participation by citizens in the political system can also be linked to the huge increase in inequalities of income and wealth in modern democracies over the last few decades – what has been termed the 'great divergence'. Voters see the rich get richer and themselves falling further behind, regardless of their voting, with the government not helping to level the playing field: so why vote? This is not only a problem for the political system, but also for the polity, for the democratic character of society.

Part of the magic formula that Tocqueville saw in America was the social equality, not only legal equality, of the populace. No one was so wealthy or so poor as to be outside the realms of society – and anyone could make it rich, to the higher end, because the ascent was not so far. Modern-day America has immense cliffs of inequality that myths of Cinderella-like rags-to-riches stories only thinly disguise. In the past large disparities of income, larger generally than in Europe, could be countered by claims that it was easier in America for people with nothing to achieve the 'American dream' of wealth and success because of America's much freer economy and society and its therefore higher social mobility. There is now less social mobility in America than there is in once 'Old World' Europe. The huge concentration of wealth and power at the very pinnacle of American society, which is increasingly self-sustaining, makes a mockery of the idea of equality of opportunity, at birth and in the marketplace.

This system might still produce immense wealth, but only for the few, and the creation of a plutocratic oligarchy is challenging Americans' ideological self-image as a democracy of equals. The vast bulk of people in the middle class or below, the 'little people', disappear from view in the political system.

▶ Wealth and power

Modern democracies generally suffer from the ancient problem of there being too much power for those with money – the plutocracy. In America, where money already had too much influence in local and federal politics, the *Citizens United* ruling of 2010 opened the floodgates for corporate money in political campaign financing. In other countries, as well, the mega-wealthy still have undue influence, partly due to their being able to finance think tanks (which inevitably favour, on average, right-wing, pro-moneyed-elite policies, although there are honourable exceptions where wealthy liberal patrons fund more inclusive, liberal research institutions). Corporations and 'media barons' have bought up newspapers and media companies with the effect of influencing the content of the political message that the media outlets give.

Influencing political discussion through media is part of civil society's control on government and a major justification for freedom of speech, and having tycoons attempt to dominate politics through the media is also not new, as the examples of William Randolph Hearst and Lord Beaverbrook show. Those examples also show, however, the potential for abuse of this freedom, and the situation recently in Italy, where Silvio Berlusconi owned most private broadcast media outlets, and as prime minister controlled their public counterparts, is not a healthy one for a democracy – for how are the voices for the other interests and opinions in the polity to be heard without adequate access to the public forum? A formal right to freedom of speech does not mean much unless there is substantial equality of rights as well to having one's argument heard by the public. The threat of media monopoly, or near monopoly, as also in the case of the Murdoch empire, is a real one for having a proper balance of democratic political debate.

▲ Silvio Berlusconi: the withering effects of plutocracy on democracy?

Partly because of plutocratic influence over much of the media and policy debates over the decades since the 'Reagan Revolution', public opinion and policy in most Western democracies have shifted to the right, especially with regard to the economy and in attitudes towards the state. This has resulted in a self-sustaining growth of capital's power and prestige. Workers have seen union rights curtailed, while the wealthy have seen their taxes slashed, and corporations have benefited from deregulation and favourable legal decisions from an increasingly conservative judiciary – at least in America, where judicial appointments are in practice political, and often partisan. Technological change, too, has transformed the workplace and the economy, making former identifications between economic function and political tendency less straightforward: blue-collar workers are no longer so dependably voters for the Left. The net effect in most Western democracies has been that the *voting* public became more right-wing – more anti-government, more conservative culturally and socially, less supportive of social solidarity (welfare), more pro-business, and more nationalistic (xenophobic).

▶ Anti-state vs. pro-state

The success of the right-wing agenda was based on being a 'popular' movement (with the support of the 'silent majority') that challenged 'liberal elites' by regaining 'freedom' of the individual from the 'nanny state'. Part of the reason for this success was that there was something to the argument, especially back in the 1970s, when the state, and state bureaucracy, held many more of the levers of power and, owing partly to technology, there were far fewer alternatives for information and interaction than there are now. A public sector that is unresponsive to the citizenry's wishes and needs, that imposes unnecessary, burdensome and inefficient regulation on society and the economy, and that is more interested in the rights and prosperity of its *own* members as opposed to the *common* good, is not serving its democratic function properly.

The old liberal argument against 'functionarism', or, as it is now known, 'bureaucracy', as the deadening hand of the governmental apparatus on the larger society, always needs to be listened to, to make sure that government is for the people, and not for itself.

Yet much of this anti-state rhetoric was wrong even then in the 1970s and is wrong now. Most Western democracies have generally honest, hard-working civil services whose aim is what it ought to be: the care for and empowerment of the populace, especially those who cannot take care of themselves or who need help to realize their potential. These civil servants generally listen to their democratically elected bosses and, while offering good policy advice, will do what their political masters tell them to do, within the bounds of good governance and the (democratic) rules. If this does not happen, the civil service is reformed, as has happened on several occasions. A well-functioning 'bureaucracy' is a vital part of modern democracy. Government, as the creation and expression of the people, has a central and very positive role to play in any democratic polity, and in suitable hands can be both liberating and equalizing in its influence on society.

The right-wing agenda has, usually deliberately, misunderstood and mischaracterized the 'nanny state' as anti-liberal and anti-democratic. In actuality, it is the right-wing agenda that has been anti-liberal *and* anti-democratic, because its freedom is the freedom of the rich and powerful to curtail the freedoms and rights of the less powerful. Its goal is to further the interests and values not of the whole people, but rather of the aristocracy of wealth and power, and the 'compact majority' that identifies itself with the ethnonational base in what are today really plural, ethnically and religiously diverse polities, not unitary nation-states. Indeed, in most modern democracies the 'compact majority' has now become a 'compact *minority*' because of the diversification of individual identity in pluralistic civil societies, together with immigration flows and secularization, especially in younger generations. The right-wing agenda claims to be about fending off the 'tyranny of the majority', but has effectively attempted to install a soft form of 'tyranny of the few'.

Fortunately for the survival of modern democracy, the right-wing agenda appears to be failing before other political, cultural, social and demographic realities. Deregulation and 'trickle-down' economics appear not to have worked as promised, and the exploitation of rights by the rich and powerful produced its own backlash. The recent attempt by the Catholic Church in America to use religious freedom as a vehicle to deny its female employees (in secular institutions such as schools and hospitals) access to contraception has come to be viewed more as an attempt of a powerful institution to deny the rights of (female) individuals. There has been a return to the perception that government and the state are a means to empower individuals, and *protect* their rights and freedoms from the powerful few, such as the wealthy and corporations.

Again, Wall Street's failures and misdemeanours in the financial crisis of 2008 helped elect a Democratic president, Barack Obama, and the rhetoric of defending the public from the machinations of an uncaring set of aristocratic plutocrats, building on the protests of the Occupy Wall Street movement, helped re-elect him. Despite Republicans' best efforts to gerrymander themselves into a permanent majority in the political system, they are now weaker than they have been for some years. Instead, a pro-government coalition of diverse minorities and women has countered the xenophobic, anti-government Tea Party, by asserting the power of the state to *protect* individual freedom from the 'compact minority' and their backers in the plutocracy. Being a pro-state liberal democrat is not a contradiction in terms. Whether this 'Obama coalition' will strengthen yet further in the next election cycle, or succumb to the greater financial muscle of the conservatives, is a key question in democracy's future. Similar battles in other democracies, notably in Hungary, are not going as well.

The recent record on how well our democracies have lived up to their own best practices is decidedly mixed. What recent political events have further shown is that the struggle to retain democratic control over plutocratic power and the nationalist 'compact minority' is no longer a domestic issue alone. The globalization of the world economy, the relatively obstacle-free ability to transfer capital around the world and to change fiscal identity almost at will (by registering a company in a tax haven, for instance), and the ability to outsource not only production but also services by the spread of the Internet and information technology, means that today's domestic political struggles inevitably have an external dimension that 'national' governments can no longer fully control, without international collaboration, or even governance. The right-wing – which wants to leave global capitalists unfettered – objects to such internationalism on *nationalist* grounds, but many also think the internationalization of democracy either impractical or inadvisable. Whether it is indeed practicable and something to work for is the next question we must address.

8

Can democracy work beyond the nation-state?

'...[T]he most sensible long-term goal for global politics remains Immanuel Kant's vision of perpetual peace under a federated, democratic world government.'

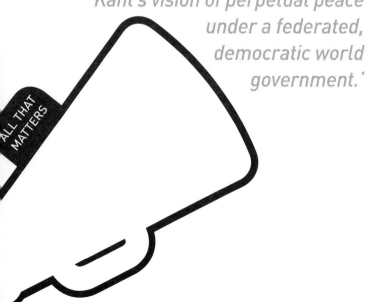

ALL THAT MATTERS

The argument about the current state of democracy points outside the nation-state, toward the transnational and global level. Questions which once appeared manageable on a domestic level now necessitate international approaches – to maintain democratic control. The relationship between capital, labour and the state, for instance, has become unbalanced because labour and the state do not have capital's access to international means. With a deregulated market economy, capital flows freely, work is offshored or outsourced, while labour has little recourse in this process, and the state either will not or cannot counter 'economic liberalism', because such measures are counterproductive or futile. The only effective response to such imbalances and resulting abuses (tax evasion via offshore tax havens, for instance) would be on a global level. In the absence of that, plutocracy, not democracy, rules.

Restoring balance in the capital–labour–state triangle requires some form of democratic governance beyond the nation-state level. Moreover, the free-riding of capital within the current system is only one transnational, border-transgressing problem facing the global community. Nuclear proliferation, population flows, the threat of global pandemics, intellectual property questions, cyber warfare, human rights, the threat of continent-wide famine, international drug and crime syndicates and networks, international terrorism, and the looming threat posed to humanity by climate change, all require solutions beyond the traditional nation-state. They require at least a *multilateral* approach from the members of the world's international community of states, but also forms of democratic involvement from the global human community. Otherwise the future of democracy, at home as well as abroad, will be in jeopardy.

Many theorists of politics, however, are sceptical of the possibility of global democratic governance. Both nationalists and many multiculturalists think such a prospect a threat to liberty, either as thinly disguised Western imperialism, or the reverse, an attack on American sovereignty (-cum-hegemony). Theorists opine that a 'democratic' world order cannot be *imposed* on the world's population and remain democratic; an unbounded entity such as 'humankind' can never have a sense of commonality without having boundaries, according to the model of the Westphalian state, with its absolute, supposedly indivisible sovereignty. Many still assume that nation-states are the 'natural communities' into which humanity is unproblematically divided. They are still stuck with G.W.F. Hegel's view that the nation-state is the highest expression of human political will, and that the only 'court of judgement' above the nation-state is 'history', the international community only ever an 'anarchic society' where might is right.

This denial of the possibility of global democratic governance is misguided. Instead, the most sensible long-term goal for global politics remains Immanuel Kant's vision of perpetual peace under a federated, democratic world government. As Kant well knew, 'the crooked timber of humanity' might cause the path thither to be less than straightforward, but there are various reasons to persist, despite the Hegelian naysayers. First, the perfect must not be made the enemy of the good. Even if getting to a perfectly equitable, responsive global democratic government structure is hard to envisage, there is no reason why there could not be practical forms of international co-operation between democracies to tackle today's pressing transnational problems.

Second, the uniform sovereign nation-state has existed more in the abstract and theory than in historical reality. Nation-states on the Westphalian model are a poor fit with actual human relations. The concept of nationality relies on an exclusive 'either/or' logic – the logic of the excluded middle – that sorts people according to one simple rule: you are either one of us, or one of them. You cannot be both. This makes no room for the multiplicity of identities and loyalties that exist in all human societies. Some people can live with this rule, being integrally of the national group. Others, with roots in more than the one nation-state, or of a religion not that of the dominant national group, or immigrants from another land, or citizens of a state who are also members of a diasporic 'nation', cannot have such an uncomplicated, conflict-free response. Their existence confounds the usual theoretical model of the simple unitary nation-state. Most polities have worked in practice according to the more liberal, inclusive logic of 'both/and' – the logic of the *included* middle. That includes the multi-national, polyglot empires of premodern history, such as the Holy Roman Empire, as well as the many dynastic, polyglot empires, such as the Habsburg Monarchy, and even the 'national' empires through which European states controlled much of the modern world, such as the British Empire. This list of 'both/and' polities also includes most successful modern democracies.

Some modern democracies appear to conform to the mono-nation-state model. A few Scandinavian countries appear ethnically homogeneous, and their sense of solidarity and their social efficiency to stem from this homogeneity. There are few other established democracies for which this has been the case. Japan is an ambivalent case. France has a linguistic mono-national identity, but it is actually immensely diverse – France as a unitary nation-state is more a product of willpower than reality. The norm, historically, has been that nation-states are composed of more than one ethnonational group. There is often a core ethnonational group, but the state's politics have revolved around that core's interactions with minorities that compose the 'nation's' actual ethnic plurality.

In some cases diversity has led to formal divisions within the bounds of the nation-state, as in the 'consociational' state of Belgium, or French-speaking Quebec within Canada. In most democracies, diversity – of religious confession, language, culture or even ethnonationality – has been the basis of the pluralism so crucial in making modern democracy 'democratic'. Switzerland is a multilingual 'nation'; from its founding the United States of America was multiethnic and multiracial and only became more so as the classic land of immigration. The United Kingdom by definition is a plural national amalgam. Traditional religious divides *constitute* a large part of national identity in states such as Germany and the Netherlands. Then there is the diversity that recent immigration has brought to much of the Western world – large Muslim minorities in Western Europe, for instance. Germany for decades has actually been a 'Germany Babylon', in Daniel Cohn-Bendit's evocative phrase. The 'nation-states' of the developing world are almost all *less* homogeneous than those of Europe. As understood as a simple, unitary national entity, the nation-state does not exist.

Third, current nation-states are already part-way to being transnational, structurally. Many democratic nation-states have strong federal elements, including most large democracies (France and Japan being the main exceptions). Within most nation-states there is considerable functional distance and complexity between the citizen's choice and the representative's political decision. With federal representative democracy, we are a long way from the narrow scope of the civic direct democracy of ancient Greece. There are now sub-continental-sized democracies such as America (315 million), Indonesia (238 million), Brazil (194 million) and India (1.2 billion). India's success demonstrates that a modern democracy is quite capable of functioning on a vast scale, and with remarkable diversity. The European Union's total population is approximately half that of India, 505 million. It should be able to have at least the same democratic input as India, national vanities and egotism notwithstanding.

Fourth, *à propos* the European Union: there are already established forms of transnational governance that satisfy many criteria of modern democracy, and could be built upon – if the member nation-states allowed it. The European Union is an immensely successful and productive transnational political entity that has brought peace and prosperity, and democracy, to most of a once war-ravaged and ideologically divided Europe. In form it has been quite democratic for many decades. There is a European Parliament; it has suffered from being the junior partner to the multilateral European Council (Council of Ministers) and the transnational executive Commission, with resulting low prestige among the European populace. European parliamentary elections produce notoriously low voter turnouts. Despite the reluctance of national governments, however, the Parliament has actually grown in power and responsibilities in recent decades.

▲ The European Parliament building: can democracy function at the supranational level?

The European Union: a model for transnational government?

Some have likened the European Union's structures to that of a 'neo-medieval' empire, and there are parallels with the Holy Roman Empire, such as the Union's polycentricity and multi-layered approach to power, and its asymmetries and exceptions when it comes to various functions and policies, such as the euro currency and the Schengen Area. These resemblances are not accidental – much of the thinking behind the Union can be traced back to the tradition of the Holy Roman Empire and the Habsburg Monarchy. The big difference is that the Union is a consensual union, based on a pooling of sovereignty of democratic polities. It is a 'bottom up' polity, where the democratically elected national governments and parliament have final say. The voting structure of the European Council is far more democratic than that of the US Senate because it is weighted to take account of population. 'Brussels' can only do what the elected governments of its constituent members agree to.

The European Union also performs a vital democratic function in the Commission's regulation of European and multinational corporations. The Commission has a history of empowering and liberating individual European consumers from the despotism of national and multinational oligopolies. Back in the 1970s the British nationalist press repeatedly complained about bureaucrats banning British culinary staples such as British ice cream, chocolate and sausages, but actually 'Brussels' was just ensuring that products in the European common market had some minimum amount of the relevant ingredient – such as cream in ice cream. The problem was there was no cream (or any dairy product) in many forms of British ice cream, only lard. The Commission was not meddling; it was protecting

British (and European) consumers from the underhand tactics of the British food industry; it was defending the powerless from the wealthy and powerful.

The same is true of the European Court of Justice, which upholds the rule of law against abuses by national governments. The independence of the European Central Bank also follows the practice of most modern democracies to keep central banks free of suborning by special interests and the party in power. The Union's insistence that new members fully take on the acquis, including many democratic rights and virtues, also shows the Union's democratic impact.

The European Union's main 'democratic deficit' has been not in actual democratic impact, but in perceptions of the European public, who view 'Brussels' as a foreign imposition and not an ally in the democratic control over their lives. Popular 'Euroscepticism' can largely be attributed to a readiness of too many politicians and national governments to use 'Europe' as a scapegoat for the problems they created, and a reluctance to let go of special national interests for the larger, European good. Britain (or rather England) has been especially reluctant to accustom itself sufficiently to the multilateralist, collaborative nature of European politics; of late, its resistance has been exacerbated by the catalyst of a set of right-wing European national governments imposing an unnecessary and irrational austerity as a result of the financial collapse of 2008. The German government, crucially, has put domestic political survival over the European common good, by indulging misguided German nationalist prejudice about 'lazy southern Europeans' even when it knows that lax policies of German financial institutions were a major factor and that financial generosity is the best antidote to market panic. Germans have not suffered much at all from the economic collapse, but over half of Spanish youth is now unemployed, a third of Italian youth; Greece remains an economic basket case. If Europe cannot deliver the goods, neither is it achieving the common good. This, not the Union's transnational democratic deficit, is what threatens its survival. Nonetheless, the Union is a far more resilient institution than it sometimes appears, because it is based on a stable equilibrium of mutual interest. If the current economic travails prove temporary, then the transnational European project will be back on track, and remain an exemplary model for other parts of the world, such as South America.

The current euro crisis should not obscure the fact that the European Union remains a great success, and shows that transnational, multilateral governance works, and can protect and enhance many aspects of democracy. The Union has encouraging lessons for democracy's prospects on a global level that need to be applied to the existing global system, for, fifth, there is already an elaborate system of global governance, with a panoply of multilateral global institutions. The question is how to make this system more democratic and more effective in combatting anti-democratic trends.

The central institution is the United Nations (UN), which has provided the framework for a legally binding international governance system since 1945. There is a long-established international legal system, with several courts based in The Hague, such as the International Court of Justice (established 1946) and the International Criminal Court (established 2002). There are also global financial and development institutions (the International Monetary Fund and

World Bank), global trade institutions (the World Trade Organization, founded 1995), and an alphabet soup of various international agencies to co-ordinate and direct global policies on many aspects of human existence: UNESCO, UNICEF, UNHCR, IAEA and WHO, to name but a few. Then there are older international organizations, predating the UN, such as the Universal Postal Union (established 1874). A vast array of international, global governance already co-ordinates and enables all the interactions that are indispensable in today's connected world of mutual interdependence. Only rogue and failed states are not tied into the economic and political international community. What needs to be done is to empower this system of global governance to support democratic states against interlopers and free riders, and to encourage the system's democratization.

Many aspects of the UN system are not democratic. France and Britain's veto power does not match modern realities; the permanent status of the United States, Russia and China is more justified, but it seems undemocratic that India, Indonesia and Brazil, and even Germany and Japan, do not have similar status. India has the same formal voting power as Nauru (population: 10,000). Major reform of the UN is needed to make it more effective and more democratic. The veto power itself is a major obstacle to the UN's practicality and, as with the experience in the European Union, will have to be amended if international governance is ever to be effectively articulated through the UN. Yet major reform of this sort is unlikely to happen unless another problem is solved: not all UN members are democracies.

Neither China nor (more ambivalently) Russia is a proper modern democracy, but both are permanent members of the UN Security Council, and many other members of the United Nations are not democracies. Therefore implementing democratic global governance remains only a goal. Yet, within these limitations, the UN system has overseen considerable advances in human rights, women's rights, economic development, the liberalizing of trade, and the establishment of the rule of law. It has also established the 'responsibility to protect' a state's population, as exercised by the international community recently in Libya. Owing to Chinese and Russian opposition, a similar fulfilling of this 'responsibility to protect' through international intervention in the Syrian crisis has not occurred, yet. But the principle is there.

Despite many flaws, the UN system fulfils many important functions, and has encouraged basic democratic principles, such as good governance, transparency, gender and racial equality, basic personal liberties, free and fair elections, religious and ethnic pluralism, and freedom from hunger and from fear. The defence of such achievements within the UN system demands constant vigilance from its democratic members, but the UN system has become more pro-democratic in recent decades, less corrupt, more accountable to the states and communities it serves. International, multilateral politics is as messy as domestic politics, but it *is* politics, and in recent years it has contributed to the common good while protecting and expanding, overall, the rights and freedoms of the world's population.

The world is today more democratic, more united and more connected than ever before. There are no huge chasms between the cultures of nations or 'civilizations'. Few parts of the human family reject the principles of the market and the necessity to trade. Adam Smith's mutual interdependence is now a global fact, and at some basic level there is a common cultural understanding of material self-betterment that belies the more extreme forms of multiculturalism. There are still large cultural differences, but the global market, the electronic global village of the Internet, and the rudiments of a system of global governance show that a pluralism premised on a common humanity within whose frame difference can be accepted is the best way of managing today's world.

The UN needs reform, but it does serve a crucial purpose. It needs strengthening for the world to face the many global problems beyond national competence. Perhaps the impetus for such reform will have to come from outside the UN system, from the Community of Democracies, or from the transnational economic organizations such as the G8 and the G20. It will only be when the members of these transnational, global forums act together to curb the excesses of global capital that democratic control over our fate can be regained.

9

Is there a future for democracy?

'The long-term prognosis for democracy is actually a positive one, if we, the people, have the political will and savvy to ensure that our elected representatives and civil servants continue to pursue the common good...'

ALL THAT MATTERS

The world is changing faster than ever, and it is unclear whether modern democracy will be able to keep up with the changes. To quote A.J.P. Taylor, 'nothing is inevitable, until it happens', and predicting democracy's future is no exception. In a world where the IT (information technology) revolution is having profound effects on the economy, society and politics, positive and negative, where inequality in the developed world is on the rise, but where millions in the developing world are rising out of poverty, where Islamic fundamentalism appears on the rise in the Islamic world, but where in other regions there is also an increase in a non-ideological, secular approach, and where over half the world's population is urban, it is hard to say what opportunities democracy will have, what threats there are to it, and whether its response will be effective. Will the connection between freedom and equality hold, or will it be broken – or will their relationship change under the pressure of new circumstance? Will democracy as we know it – a hybrid of government by elected officials, a free market economy and the rule of law – nevertheless survive in recognizable form?

▶ The Arab Spring

In some parts the prospects for democracy have never been brighter, but in others there have rarely been so many problems and doubts about its effectiveness, especially in dealing with inequality, economic distress, and global issues. The focus of democratic interest has recently been on the Arab

Spring. The lessons for democracy are so far mixed, its prospects here ambivalent. On the one hand, the initial revolutions in North Africa benefited greatly from new communications technology, which made it almost impossible to stop information getting out and being shared, allowing for greater co-ordination by the revolutionaries. On the other hand, technology has done little to solve old problems of political organization and economic disorder. It has not enabled the initial revolutionaries, often young, quite secular professionals, to achieve political power, once more established, less progressive, elements in society came into play, such as the Muslim Brotherhood in Egypt. As in 1848, the idealistic optimism of the revolutions' beginnings has had to face social and economic realities that militate against Western democratic values.

To some commentators, it must look as though the move to 1849, the year of reaction, has already repeated itself. The rule of a fairly pragmatic Islamist, President Morsi, in Egypt was not in itself cause for democratic despair, if he had followed the model, for instance, of the moderate Islamist government of Turkey. Instead, the army's intervention in Egypt has been justified on the grounds that Morsi was pushing the Islamist agenda too far, in an anti-democratic manner. The fact that Turkish prime minister Recep Tayyip Erdoğan also seems to be overstepping the bounds of the status quo with Turkey's secular establishment also suggests the problems in keeping the tension between Islamist politics and modern democracy under control. The catastrophe in Syria should concentrate minds on the need for practical and moderate policies, but history is littered with examples of people not learning the obvious lessons. One of them appears to be Morsi; Erdoğan might be another. Certainly, the post-revolutionary governments of the Arab Spring seem so far, with the possible exception of Tunisia, incapable of producing effective governance. The potential extension of Iranian Islamic fundamentalism's influence in Iraq, Lebanon, the Gulf and Palestine, through Hezbollah and Hamas, also should not be discounted as an anti-democratic factor. Having democracy's supporters side with Saudi Arabia, an absolute theocratic monarchy, is frankly a peculiar outcome, but perhaps the most practical.

▶ Prospects in South America and Africa

South America has been lately a success story for democracy. The right-wing dictatorships that so recently dominated the continent have gone. Chile, Brazil and Uruguay have confidently returned to the democratic community, and the recent Brazilian riots do not appear to change this trajectory. There are several countries, led by the late Hugo Chavez's Venezuela, which have promoted 'Bolivarian' democracy, putting the popular element in modern democracy ahead of its more liberal and market-oriented aspects. Argentina has also pursued an independent course that veers from the modern democratic model, especially regarding financial rules. On the other hand, these countries maintain democratic forms and will probably come to resemble the other modern democracies on the continent. Then there is Cuba, a souvenir of the Cold War, still exerting a sentimental (anti-American) influence over many Central and South Americans. Yet it is likely that the Cuban regime will liberalize in the not-too-distant future and join most of the rest of the Caribbean and Central American states as functioning democracies; one hopes that includes Haiti at last. Mexico, once only formally a democratic republic, has made great advances in democratization and, despite its drug-cartel problems, is set to be a major player in pan-American politics. Assuming economic growth continues to be adequate, the prospects for democracy in Central and South America appear good.

Sub-Saharan Africa offers a better prospect for democratic progress than it has for some time, but it is still halting. Ghana, Benin, South Africa, Botswana, Zambia and Namibia counted as 'flawed democracies' in the Democracy Index of 2011, and a more generous definition of modern democracy would include more states, such as Nigeria, Liberia, Tanzania and Senegal, perhaps Kenya, too, after the recent election there. Much of the continent is still struggling to achieve sustainable democratic norms along with general economic prosperity. For every Ghana, there is a Zimbabwe, or Democratic Republic of Congo – and even a state regarded as democratic in 2011, such as Mali, can quickly fall back to more discouraging forms of governance. Relatively prosperous countries such as South Africa are often the objects of Western investor scepticism, but South Africa continues to be democratic; Ghanaian success also suggests a democratic way forward. On the transnational level, the African Union has also proved quite active and responsible in its responses to the continent's many crises. Post-colonial legacies are waning as an obstacle to co-operation and more free-market economic policies, so sub-Saharan Africa could become a more positive area for modern democracy.

▶ Asia – the crux of democracy

The future of democracy will likely be decided in Asia. If India can continue to flourish as a democracy, this will be a vital support for the democratic cause. It might well spread its democratic influence further afield, to Sri Lanka, Bangladesh and a newly receptive Burma, although nothing would be more helpful for India than peace with Pakistan, and for that country to solidify its democratic credentials and defuse the threat of Islamic fundamentalism. Most south-east Asian states, even Malaysia, seem well on the way to being prosperous and influential democracies. Singapore has been so successful as to be a model for a sort of economically neoliberal authoritarianism, but it has shown democratizing tendencies of late and could without much difficulty join those other major democracies in the region: Japan, South Korea, Taiwan, Australia and New Zealand.

The big question is what will happen in China, with its 1.4 billion people. It is, formally, a 'people's republic' but this still means a state ruled absolutely by a dirigiste oligarchy, the Communist Party. China's recent economic success has prompted many Chinese and others to see it as a superior, more efficient model for generating economic growth and hence wellbeing – at the expense of personal freedom. The actual net effect of China's prosperity could well be that the new middle classes will demand more power for civil society outside the party apparatus, much as happened in nineteenth-century central Europe. Or perhaps the politics already practised within the party will simply externalize itself and form a competitive political party system out of the body of the party itself – as party leaders appeal increasingly to the interests and approval of the public at large. China will, I think, soon enough, within a generation, become a *form* of modern democracy, and at that point an already fairly pragmatic leadership will be more persuadable as a partner in global multilateral governance.

▲ The 'Goddess of Democracy': the Tiananmen Square protests in Beijing, China in 1989

Russia seems to be going the other way, back to older soviet or even tsarist forms. If the West resumes economic growth, however, Russian geopolitical power and the prestige of its neo-authoritarian style should diminish and the other side of Russia – the wish to be part of the free West – will reassert itself, akin to Ukraine's effort to strengthen contacts with the EU. Once Russia liberalizes, its remaining allies in eastern Europe and Eurasia will perforce do so also. It is a matter of when – *if* the West resumes growth and stays on its democratic course.

▶ European democracy in the balance

That is a bigger 'if' than it should be. The current economic doldrums in Europe have been unnecessarily exacerbated by bad policy decisions, such as the insistence, led by Germany but echoed by Britain and others, on austerity, and the unwelcome return of narrow-minded interpretations of national interests. The economic travails have produced, among other things, the current Hungarian government of Viktor Orbán. Democratically elected by a massive landslide in 2010, his Fidesz party has used its absolute control of Hungary's political system to compromise many of the liberal-democratic features of the Hungarian state. A democratically elected party is pursuing deeply anti-democratic measures in the heart of Europe. The crisis caused by Jörg Haider in Austria in 2000 is child's play compared to Orbán's policies in Hungary. If the European Union's other members cannot counter Orbán's power grab, then many of the assumptions of Europe being a community of democracies will be upended. Meanwhile, Germany's government appears to think that outrageous levels of unemployment in southern European countries, which also have anti-democratic traditions, are quite acceptable in pursuit of economic virtue. No wonder Europe has lost the optimistic energy it possessed during the enlargement of 2004.

The current German-led policy of austerity being followed to solve Europe's fiscal and economic crisis has the potential to break the Union in the longer term, because of the resentments it inevitably causes. It is unwise for future European solidarity, and even anti-democratic in its doctrinaire refusal to compromise, insisting on the necessity of such massive economic pain. A better policy would be to realize that economics is not a zero-sum game, and that combining greater mutual dependence with more generous financial help from the European Central Bank and deficit spending would produce greater economic growth and more financial confidence (as the American recovery has shown). Keynesian economics is much better suited to democracy than the current rigid neoliberal policies, not only because it avoids unnecessary hardship in the populace, but it also allows for more positive government action. The German, and even more inexcusably the British, governments' rejection of Keynesianism is tragic.

▶ Threats to democracy

The economic crisis has also undermined Europe's pluralist embrace of diversity. It has exacerbated the very nationalism and xenophobia that partly caused it (through inadequately co-ordinated transnational responses to the financial collapse). Right-wing media corporations, their billionaire owners and their political allies have, moreover, stoked and then exploited fear of immigrants, especially Islamophobia against the many Muslim immigrants now in such countries as France, Germany and the Netherlands. This in turn was partly a reaction to another major threat to democracy, the Islamist terrorism of al-Qaeda and its affiliated jihadists, post-9/11. This growth in Islamophobia has also had a large impact in America. It might even be said that the threat of terrorism in the West is not as much of a potential long-term threat to democratic values as the Islamophobic paranoia that it has evoked as a response, especially in the rush to curtail civil liberties in favour of security and order.

There has been a justified counter-reaction to the curtailing of many individual rights when it comes to terrorism, and the expansion of the surveillance and control apparatus of the state. The Guantanamo Bay Detention Camp remains a dagger at the heart of civil liberties and the rule of law, and it is unnerving to think that the Internet is full of snoops. The ability of drones to 'take out' terrorist suspects from thousands of feet in the sky, controlled by someone thousands of miles away is also repugnant to our sense of fair play and personal freedom. Yet the libertarian paranoia created by the realization that one cannot evade the state any more is itself misguided. New technology has made the world smaller and increased the reach of the law and government, regardless of our ideological reluctance. There is no public space in Britain not under video surveillance; in the United States, the open frontier of the Wild West has effectively disappeared, as surveillance and communication technology has progressed and we are ever more dependent on the Internet – which, as the recent irresponsible revelations by Edward Snowden have shown (are we surprised?), is monitored, at varying degrees, by the intelligence services of our governments.

Physical freedom can no longer exist without democracy's institutional defences of *legal* freedoms, and controls on government. It is often not even government that is the threat – it is private snooping, by the newspapers of News Corporation, for instance, that recently posed threats to privacy; the only defence against such intrusions is the state, *even* when they potentially come from the state itself. That, ironically, is the conclusion to be drawn from the Snowden affair – the surveillance that he revealed was not only hard to prevent in our current wired world; it was also justifiable, even, perhaps, necessary. The key point is that the government agencies are under a tight legal regimen, reinforced and expanded by the Obama administration, which has so far prevented – as far as we know – any major abuse by government agents and agencies. We have available legal and political measures by which we can control the new threats to our democratic liberties. As citizens of a democracy, we just need to be vigilant in demanding their enforcement, and make sure that the people we entrust with these powers understand and act on their responsibilities to that democracy.

▶ Democracy and the new media

New technology is already having far-reaching effects on another vital aspect of democracy: freedom of speech and the free media. In many respects information technology and the Internet have enabled an explosion of free speech and have been instrumental in democratization. The liberating effect of citizens being able to participate in discussions and co-ordinate action not only on a national but also transnational and global level is incalculable. The Internet has been a boon for our 'monitory democracy', where NGOs and almost spontaneously formed pressure groups can keep a critical eye on power. Yet there is also a danger in this flood of information: the lack of gate-keepers means that we no longer have an institutional adjudication of what is true or just politicized slur. Before, 'newspapers-of-record' or broadcast news could be relied on to tell us something close to objective truth. We could obtain well-founded opinion from the 'op-ed' pages of newspapers. *The Guardian* and *The Daily Telegraph* had their respective ideological preferences, but both were within the same, respectable political universe. In the chaotic, open world of today's Web, there is not the same reliability, yet the dependable organs of public opinion, the major newspapers and broadcast stations, are being increasingly undermined by this same virtual world, when they are not being suborned by their corporate paymasters. If we lose these anchors of the public forum, as is quite possible given market trends, the danger is that 'public opinion' will be open to manipulation of rumour and hearsay because of *too much* information, rather than too little.

Yet it is also possible that the Internet will become more reliable and less open to abuse, either due to cannier consumers, self-regulation or regulation by democratically elected governments, domestically and transnationally. The Internet is not independent of private or public institutions – just as with the world financial system, it would not exist without innumerable technical conventions and rules, and there are already signs of how access can be controlled and supervised, if necessary. The trick is to make sure such control, domestic and global, is democratic and liberal, not that of an authoritarian power such as China, or – Edward Snowden and Julian Assange's wish for asylum notwithstanding – enemies of the free media such as Venezuela and Ecuador.

▶ A positive prognosis

The long-term prognosis for democracy is actually a positive one, if we, the people, have the political will and savvy to ensure that our elected representatives and civil servants continue to pursue the common good rather than that of special interests or themselves. The economic crisis has tested transnational and national governance in Europe, and many in the political class and even the electorate have failed (witness the bizarre Italian election in February 2013). Yet Europe is still standing, and despite the execrable levels of unemployment around the Mediterranean, violent resistance or protest against governments or Europe has been remarkably mild. Those affected appear to have decided that accepting the social bargain of democracy – on a national and European level – is still the one most likely to produce the most common (and individual) good, in the long run. That patience is not infinite, but so far it has held – it needs to be rewarded with jobs and prosperity. There has to be a remedy for Europe's *nationally* articulated inequalities, as well as for the domestic increase in inequality that European states share with most other Western democracies, most notably the United States. In Europe, national *special* interests must not be put before the transnational solidarity that will benefit the *common* good.

On a domestic and global level, it bears repeating, democracies need to reassert control over money and capital, whether this means capping bankers' bonuses, transaction taxes, or cracking down on tax havens and tax loopholes. Financial and fiscal discipline should be enforced for long-term economic benefit, but with consideration of social justice and equity. The public good ultimately comes before the rights of creditors. Bankers and the financial sector should be the servants of the public, not their masters – otherwise democracy succumbs to plutocracy.

Much of the story outside of Europe and the West is one of continuing improvement in the standard of living and the booming of the middle class, which means democracy will likely expand. In the West, economic recovery will most likely confirm or restore the faith of the voters in their democratic systems. The survival of democracy is, however, not a given. We cannot rely solely on objective protections to save our democracy from ourselves, especially in societies with vast economic and social inequalities. We need to ensure that there is a place for the democratic popular will – our will – to assert itself where appropriate, in defending the people, and their democracies, from the threats that they face in a rapidly changing world, both internationally and domestically. The answer to the threat to democracies from without, especially financial and economic forces beyond national control, would be the provision of some sort of international level of democratic control; and the answer to the threat from within, especially vast inequalities in income and hence in power, would be a greater assertion of each society's control over its collective human and capital resources. Both, as we have seen, are possible. It just takes the political will of the people to make sure they occur.

10

Conclusion: Why we should care about democracy

'Modern democracy's main concern is the empowerment of each individual citizen to realize his or her human dignity.'

As will have become clear, democracies do not always live up to their best practices, and have many flaws. This leaves democracy as a governing principle open to many doubts and criticisms as to whether it can really deliver the common good. One of the biggest frustrations for democracy's supporters in principle is that governments legitimately chosen by the electorate often do not follow the wise path of policy, preferring to indulge either the delusions of their constituents or the wishes of (wealthy and hence powerful) special interests. In the case of the response of the American political class to the threat of climate change, both of these bad motives appear to have come into play, interacting with the preference for inertia in the American constitutional system to produce a completely inadequate response to this dire threat to our existence. Even though the 'government', the Obama administration, tries its best to combat climate change, it is severely hampered by the Republican opposition to such policies, and their ability to achieve stasis in the legislative branch of the same government.

Were this to continue, the old fears of liberals such as Mill and Bagehot that democracy is incapable of producing responsible policy because the electorate and the system are not up to the task would be tragically confirmed. As another former liberal, Churchill, put it: 'The best argument against democracy is a five-minute conversation with the average voter.' On the other hand, most of the political pressure to address climate change has come from other democracies and from NGOs in those countries and in the United States. The staunchest opponents of efforts against greenhouse gas emissions control have included non-democratic countries such as China, and it is not at all clear that democracies have responded worse that non-democracies. Indeed, the reverse appears true – the need to respond to climate change has emerged from democratic civil society. It may be an inadequate response, but there is hope that it will soon improve, if electoral pressure on the (American) political class is increased, and it is better than that of non-democracies, overall. So we are back to that other quote from our reluctant democrat: 'No one pretends that democracy is perfect or all-wise. Indeed, it has been said that democracy is the worst form of government except all those other forms that have been tried from time to time.'

▶ Proof by subtraction

One of the most effective ways of showing why we should care about democracy remains Churchill's proof by subtraction. Most of the alternatives either have lost any legitimacy they once possessed (theocracy, divine-right absolute monarchy, aristocratic republic), have been shown not to work very well (authoritarian dictatorship, imperialism, nationalism, corporatism, technocracy, socialist one-party rule), or have been shown to have horrendous, evil consequences (fascism, communism).

Even those such as Singapore's neoliberal technocracy end up creating a society that chafes under its rule, and to which it ceases to be responsive enough, leading to the perceived need to... democratize. Libertarian pipe dreams of a civil society (economy) without democratic political control do not work because a purely market-based system does not recognize the 'externalities' that the public needs to flourish as a society, which only the people choosing as voters, and not consumers, can reasonably know. Capitalism, the market-and-property-based economy, is a necessary component of modern democracy, but it has to be kept in balance with the other aspects: individual rights, equality and popular self-government, which the market cannot itself provide. Experience has shown that the political world should normally defer to the market when setting prices, but also that the market should defer to the political world when setting public policy beyond the market's ken. The market might manage to aggregate the sum of individual interests, but it cannot know the public, common good. Regimes imposed by force to uphold special interests of one sort or another also do not work in the long run, as they run into resistance (active or passive) of those forced to satisfy the benefit and will of others. China, as mentioned, is often cited as a counter-model, but it lacks credibility on many levels – not least, who really believes in communism in the Chinese Communist Party today? This explains its adoption of nationalist rhetoric, but the regime is ideologically hollow and, without the authority that comes from a higher ideological credo, will probably change functionally into a form of democratic system.

There are still large parts of the world in which forms of theocracy still outcompete democracy, especially in the Islamic world, and even in 'Islamic republics' that otherwise claim to be democratic. But theocracy and democracy do not mix well. The relationship between religion and democracy has always been complicated. There have been many claims for various religions as having contributed to the development and success of democracy. Judaism, primitive Christianity and various forms of Protestantism have received particular attention in this respect, and even Catholicism has had its advocates as a source of democracy, owing to the Thomist traditions of natural law and conciliarism, among other aspects. That has not prevented most established forms of the same religions from being strongly anti-democratic in their governing structures, or in their illiberal suppression of any form of dissent as heresy. Judaism is a partial exception here, but largely because, as the religion of a diasporic group, it was hardly ever in an established status.

Fortunately for democracy's sake (and partly a cause of modern democracy's success), the main Western religions eventually came to a compromise with democracy, the state and each other, so that now religion is largely a neutralized issue in a secular political system. As a part of this compromise, religious groups changed from trying to impose their values and beliefs on others through electoral power, to seeing their religion as a source of democratic and pluralist values. Among Catholics, for instance, there was a profound change, guided by the thought of figures such as Jacques Maritain and John Courtney Murray, towards an acceptance of pluralist democracy, as embodied in Vatican II. *Christian* democracy changed its emphasis to Christian *democracy*, accepting of the secular political and social, pluralist world. Despite some backsliding this acceptance of de facto separation of the secular political realm from the religious sphere, even in countries which retain established churches, has held. Even so, blasphemy is still a crime in many Western democracies, and was abolished in the UK only in 2008. Religiously informed issues, such as abortion and gay marriage, remain central to political discourse in the United States, despite the constitutional separation of church and state.

The main hope for relations between democracy and the Islamic world is that a similar accommodation between religion and a secular political world, which accepts religious pluralism even in a society with a dominant religious group can be effected in Muslim states as it was in Christian-majority ones. Experience would suggest that this is more than possible: Turkey and Indonesia would seem to function quite well as secular democracies with a predominantly Muslim population. The occasional problem over the attire of Western pop stars is not much different from similar problems among more conservative communities in Western democracies. Problems arise when a Muslim majority in a state insists on making Islam the established religion in the old style, with severe punishment of slights to religious faith and sensitivities and a denial of civil equality with those of other religions, or of gender equality because of supposed religious precepts. When blasphemy is still punishable by death in a state, that is not a democracy. Nor is it a democracy in our meaning when women are not allowed to be educated or to wear what attire *they* choose. (Conversely, banning the hijab is also an attack on pluralism and hence anti-democratic.) If there are 'Islamic democracies' that tolerate or even embrace such laws and policies – even if a majority of the electorate approves of them – they are not democracies. Religious pluralism and gender equality are necessary parts of modern democracy.

▶ A community of free individuals

The only political tradition that manages to include the whole population in participating in their own government, and yet protects the freedoms of every individual citizen to live their life as they see fit, is modern democracy. That is because that is what it was developed to do – modern democracy is *essentially* pragmatic, and its practical nature, as a system of pure politics, is one of its great strengths. This is not mere empirical accident – democracy also benefits from fitting so well with the basic structures of human experience.

Schelling's theory of salience

One way of thinking of this is through Thomas Schelling's theory of salience, which shows how people can come to an understanding without communication. For instance, two parachutists have landed and want to meet; they cannot communicate with each other, but they both have maps of the terrain, and so can figure out that the best place to meet is at the bridge over the river, because that is the *salient* point, that leaps out from the landscape.

Similarly, in political organization there are various aspects to the human landscape, various types of categories, relationships and units, such as family, ethnicity, gender, religious affiliation and hierarchy, economic function or business corporations, levels of wealth or of rank, but each is either too contentious, too indefinite, too changeable, too compromised, or too partial to be a basis of mutual agreement for how society is to be governed; whereas everyone, almost by definition, can see individuals as distinct units, salient points in the human landscape, and agree on the concept of the individual as the self-determining, rational actor in the market and the polis. The individual (with his/her rights, choices, needs and desires) is thus the basic institution of modern democracy, which surpasses those other aspects to the landscape.

Democracy is the form of government based on the concept of society and the polis as a community of free individuals. It therefore avoids the reification (mistaking a man-made concept or institution as an independent, objective, *real* thing) that most other governmental forms fall into – for instance 'Christendom', 'the state', 'the market', 'the nation' or even 'the people' and 'society'. Instead, democracy ultimately denies that there is anything in the political world greater than 'us'. Theodor Herzl once put the basic democratic insight very succinctly: 'I do not belong to my fatherland; my fatherland belongs to me.' It is essentially the same thought behind Woody Guthrie's ode to the democratic potential of America:

'This Land is Your Land'. Actually, democracy does not need land as such; indeed, on a global level we do belong to the planet, just as, increasingly, the planet is our responsibility. Where these quotes are so insightful is in their idea that the governmental structures that control the territory, the states in which we live, are *ours*. We do not belong to the state, for we, as citizens, are the state's stakeholders, each of us, equally – in a democracy.

Modern democracy's main concern is the empowerment of each individual citizen to realize his or her human dignity. The idea of dignity for all is in one sense a complete contradiction in terms, for dignity was once the respect deriving from *rank*, in a hierarchical or caste society. When *everyone* has rank, there is no rank left – but democratic dignity is, in effect, levelling up, not down. The secret of democracy's attractiveness, in the past and today, is not only that it has provided material wellbeing, but also that it provides the sense of self-worth that Tocqueville described in the social equality of the young United States. We have been concerned many times in this book with the relationship of society and the state, the individual and the state, but democracy is first and foremost a relationship that exists between each individual member of the community. Liberty and equality are the main drivers of the democratic experience, but what holds it together is *fra*-ternity – the power between individuals that ties them together (regardless of gender), not as members of an ethnic group, or a nation, but as individual human beings in a political community.

Enabling the 'good life'

Beyond all the arguments about democracy's practicality, there is a strong moral argument for it. It is the best way of combining Aristotle's insight that Man is a 'political animal', destined and programmed to live in a society (social contract or no) with other human beings in pursuit of the common good, with Kant's concept of humanity as a kingdom of ends, each individual being one of those ends, each free and equal with all others. Or, to put it in more quotidian language, it achieves both the co-operation of individuals for mutual benefit, and their getting along with each other in mutual respect (as Rodney King might have put it). One can derive from this combination also a very powerful duty that democracy imposes on its individual members: the civic duty of active participation in the polis. For, if the greatest description of democracy's principles was Thomas Jefferson's claims to 'life, liberty and the pursuit of happiness', the deeper meaning of the last concept is the same as Aristotle's 'pursuit of the good life', and a central part of the good life, as a political animal, was the individual's participation in the polis's self-government. Democracy allows individuals to be fully human in a way provided by no other governmental form. Serving on a jury or voting is not only an imposed duty, but also an exercise in self-government, in liberty. Public service in a democracy, and even being a politician, is, despite all appearances, a highly moral calling.

Modern democracy in practice combines all sorts of other forms. It is, as stated before, a hybrid system. There are very strong elements of aristocracy (we choose our representatives, I hope, on who is *best* for the job), bureaucracy, plutocracy and technocracy. If a modern democracy does not respect science and specialized expertise, and does not give the state some role as a tutelary state that can educate the populace to be good and competent citizens, then it will no longer find itself providing the common good. Scepticism is a powerful democratic value, and there have been times when politicians and the public would have been wise to question scientific 'truth', but this can be overdone. Empirical acceptance of the evidence is also a strong democratic value – it is the art of politics, and politicians, to judge when the scientists and experts are in fact right, about climate change, for instance, and to persuade a sceptical public of that fact. But that is what freedom of speech, the arts of rhetoric and the public space of civil society are for, in a functioning democracy.

Modern democracy also fulfils the two goals that John Stuart Mill set for representative government: it is able to work with people as they are (Churchill's average voter), and, despite the occasional setback and frustration, improve them. Democracy is at its best when it is not only a means to the end of efficient provision of social goods for its members, but also the provider of the common good in a higher sense, of enabling its citizens to become the mature and responsible participants in the good life that has been the aim of politics since Aristotle.

Democracy is a learning process, where people learn by participation, in self-government but also in the public debate with which all policy should be accompanied. The question we are now faced with is whether we, as parts of a global human community, can learn quickly enough to respond adequately to our current predicaments. In our globalized world – where the world's resources are so unequally shared, and its environment so exploited and abused as to be soon, if the scientific community is to be believed, so harshly degraded as to be barely inhabitable – can citizens learn the limits of their power in the face of the laws of nature, but the extent of their responsibility, and their power, when it comes to the social, economic and political world – the world created by human beings? Will we recognize our social responsibility to others, and ourselves, and our power, through our current democracies, and international democratic institutions yet to be created, to achieve social justice by controlling the plutocratic trend to inequality of the market economy? Will we recognize our responsibility to ourselves and the Earth's other living creatures to brake and reverse the consequences of our, humanity's, role as the Sorcerer's Apprentice of climate change? Democracy, as the product of centuries of human intelligence and human political will, sometimes looks as though it is not up to the job, but there are no better solutions, and we can but hope that the learning curve of our citizenries will catch up with the breakneck speed of modern change. What should be clear from what has gone before is that the best solution to the world's problems today is, both on the domestic level and on the global level, more democracy, not less.

This 100 Ideas section gives ways you can explore the subject in more depth. It's much more than just the usual reading list.

100 IDEAS

Five sites of democratic memory

1   Runnymede: a meadow along the Thames in Surrey, England, where Magna Carta was supposedly sealed in 1215. Although it is unclear where exactly in the area the historic event took place, several memorials celebrate this site as the source of the Anglo-American 'democratic' tradition.

2   Independence Hall, Philadelphia: the revered site of the signing of the Declaration of Independence of 4 July 1776, and of the Constitutional Convention of 1786–87. A visit to the Pennsylvania State House across the way is also worthwhile – in the State House are the images of four people that Pennsylvanians thought fundamental to the success of the American Revolution: George Washington, Benjamin Franklin, Louis XVI and… Marie Antoinette.

3   **Versailles Tennis Court:** the site of the Bastille in Paris (now marked by a large monument) is easier to get to, and more famous, but this is where the revolution really began, with the 'Tennis Court Oath' of the members of the Third Estate/ National Assembly on 20 June 1789.

4   **Wenceslas Square, Prague:** the site of the Czechoslovak 'Velvet Revolution', a major part of the 'turn' of 1989, which freed East Central Europe from communist rule under the hegemony of the Soviet Union. Václav Havel, a writer and dissident, and one of the revolution's leaders, later became president of Czechoslovakia (and then president of the Czech Republic).

5   **Robben Island, South Africa:** tours can be taken to view the prison island and the prison cell where the greatest hero of democracy of recent decades, Nelson Mandela, spent 18 years of the 27 years of his imprisonment under the apartheid regime.

Five introductions

6   *Democracy: A Very Short Introduction*, by Bernard Crick (Oxford University Press)

7   *On Democracy*, by Robert A. Dahl (Yale University Press)

8   *Democracy Ancient and Modern*, by M.I. Finley (Rutgers University Press)

9   *The Life and Death of Democracy*, by John Keane (Pocket Books)

10 *On Politics*, by Alan Ryan (Liveright Publishing Corporation)

Ten films

11 *Mr. Smith Goes to Washington* (1939): the classic (and somewhat cynical) view of how American democracy actually works.

12 *The Great Dictator* (1940): its finale is one of the greatest speeches on democracy ever made, in reality or fiction.

13 *Passport to Pimlico* (1949): a post-war British take on the notion of popular sovereignty.

14 *Twelve Angry Men* (1957): a searing look at how citizens actually make decisions (as jurors).

15 *Blazing Saddles* (1974): Mel Brooks's comic genius manages to make a Western into a paean to liberal pluralism, and a critique of populist racism and the corruption of politics by capitalism.

16 *Lawrence of Arabia* (1962): one example of how Romantic nationalism and democracy don't always work well together.

17 *Gandhi* (1982): how nationalist democracy overcame imperialism, and the consequences.

18 *Invictus* (2009): how democracy triumphantly manipulated nationalism for the common good.

19 *Django Unchained* (2012): a moving, romanticized (ultra-violent) fantasy of how the true values of democracy won out over slavery.

20 *Lincoln* (2012): a portrayal of the political reality of how the true values of democracy won out over slavery.

Ten classics

21 *The Politics*, by Aristotle (*c.*350 BCE)

22 *Two Treatises of Government*, by John Locke (1689)

23 *The Wealth of Nations*, by Adam Smith (1776)

24 *The Federalist Papers*, by Alexander Hamilton, James Madison and John Jay (1787–88)

25 *Perpetual Peace*, by Immanuel Kant (1795)

26 *Democracy in America*, by Alexis de Tocqueville (1835–40)

27 *Considerations on Representative Government*, by John Stuart Mill (1861)

28 *The Open Society and its Enemies*, by Karl Popper (1943)

29 *Four Essays on Liberty*, by Isaiah Berlin (1958/1969)

30 *In Defence of Politics*, by Bernard Crick (1962)

Five TV series

31 *Yes Minister / Yes, Prime Minister* (1980–87): the comic version of how politics in a democracy works.

32 *House of Cards* (UK: 1990–95; US: 2013–): the tragic version of how politics in a democracy works.

33 *The West Wing* (1999–2006): how American liberals think democracy works.

34 *Star Trek* (1966–69): how American liberals used to think democracy would work in the future.

35 *Till Death Us Do Part* (1965–75) / *All in the Family* (1971–79): why democracy still has some work cut out for it.

Five documentaries

36 *The Loving Story* (2012): how an ordinary couple brought the ban on interracial marriage in Virginia to an end – in *1967*.

37 *Eyes on the Prize* (1987–90): 14 hours on the history of the Civil Rights Movement in the USA.

38 *The War Room* (1993): behind the scenes in a political campaign (Clinton's in 1992).

39 *And the Pursuit of Happiness* (1986): Louis Malle's wide-ranging depiction of the diversity of the immigrant experience in America in the 1980s.

40 *Inside Job* (2010): how the 'masters of the universe' failed the people.

Ten more texts for thinking about democracy

41 *Cosmopolitanism*, by Kwame Anthony Appiah (Norton)

42 *Visions of World Community*, by Jens Bartelson (Cambridge University Press)

43 *Making Our Democracy Work*, by Stephen Breyer (Vintage)

44 *We Hold These Truths*, by John Courtney Murray (Rowman & Littlefield)

45 *What's the Matter with Kansas? How Conservatives Won the Heart of America*, by Thomas Frank (Holt McDougal)

46 *The Foundations of Modern Political Thought*, by Quentin Skinner (Cambridge University Press)

47 *The Great Divergence*, by Timothy Noah (Bloomsbury Press)

48 *A Theory of Justice*, by John Rawls (Belknap Press)

49 *The Idea of Justice*, by Amartya Sen (Belknap Press)

50 *Europe as Empire*, by Jan Zielonka (Oxford University Press)

Five musicals

51 *Les Misérables* (1980): a failed French revolution (1832) becomes the embodiment of the romance of all revolution?

52 *South Pacific* (1949): both a testament to the power of democracy at war, and an evisceration of the racism that still accompanied it.

53 *Hairspray: The Musical* (2002): how (young) people overcame bigotry and racism by dancing (and marching). Much more intelligent than it sounds.

54 *West Side Story* (1957): what happens when diversity is not modulated by pluralism.

55 *Urinetown* (2001): the horrors of Thatcherism/Reaganism, but with an environmentalist twist.

Five musical pieces to be democratic by

56 'Ode to Joy', from the Ninth Symphony, by Ludwig van Beethoven (1824): among many other things, now the anthem of the European Union.

57 Symphony No. 9 in E minor, *From the New World*, by Antonin Dvořák (1893): the musical counterpart of *Democracy in America*.

58 'Jupiter', from *The Planets*, by Gustav Holst (1914): written at the beginning of the First World War, the war 'to make the world safe for democracy'. In 1921, Holst set the poem 'I vow to thee my country' to the music of 'Jupiter' and the resulting hymn has subsequently become a standard of Remembrance Day (Armistice) ceremonies and celebrations of the British defence of democracy.

59 *Rhapsody in Blue*, by George Gershwin (1924), arranged by Duke Ellington (1932): jazz, developed largely by African Americans and Jewish Americans, has been seen as America's major cultural contribution – a democratic musical form, based on the equality of the players and accommodating their freedom of expression. Jazz has proved remarkably adaptable to other cultures as well, so that it is now seen as the *international* musical form as well. UNESCO now sponsors an International Jazz Day: 30 April.

60 *Fanfare for the Common Man*, by Aaron Copland (1942): written to support the American effort in the war (the Second World War) that really did make the world safe(r) for democracy.

Five songs of democracy

61 'Jerusalem', by William Blake and Hubert Parry (1916): another product of the First World War, but also sung now annually at the UK Labour Party Conference.

62 'This Land is Your Land', by Woody Guthrie (1940): a classic statement of the basic democratic principle. Two original verses from 1940, critical about the American reality about property and hunger, were dropped from the 1944 version but have subsequently been reclaimed.

63 'We Shall Overcome', by C.A. Tindley and Z. Horton (1947): the anthem of the Civil Rights Movement – invariably sung at commemorations on Martin Luther, Jr. King Day (third Monday in January).

64 'Nkosi Sikelel' iAfrika' (1897), performed by Ladysmith Black Mambazo (2006): the anthem of the African National Congress, and the main part of the official anthem of the new South Africa. The melody is from the hymn tune 'Aberystwyth', by Joseph Parry, 1879.

65 'Man in the Mirror', by Michael Jackson (1988): Michael Jackson, really? But listen to the words.

Ten novels

66 *Half of a Yellow Sun*, by Chimamanda Ngozi Adichie (Harper, 2007)

67 *To Kill a Mockingbird*, by Harper Lee (Arrow, 2010 [1960])

68 *A Tale of Two Cities*, by Charles Dickens (Wordsworth Editions, 1999 [1859])

69 *White Teeth*, by Zadie Smith (Penguin, 2000)

70 *The White Tiger*, by Aravind Adiga (Atlantic, 2009)

71 *The Plague*, by Albert Camus (Penguin, 2002 [1947])

72 *The Lord of the Flies*, by William Golding (Faber, 1997 [1959])

73 *The Grapes of Wrath*, by John Steinbeck (Penguin, 1970 [1959])

74 *The Plot against America*, by Philip Roth (Vintage, 2005)

75 *Animal Farm*, by George Orwell (Penguin, 2013 [1945]). In fact, anything by Orwell – for example, *Essays* (Penguin, 2000). 'Shooting an Elephant' is a must-read for any democrat.

Five (more) quotations relevant to democracy

76 'As I would not be a slave, so I would not be a master.' Abraham Lincoln (1 August 1858)

77 'The Venetians, in their time, used to say that they did not wish for Austria to govern them well – it should not govern them at all.' Berthold Molden (6 July 1914)

78 'The only tyrant I accept in this world is the "still small voice" within me. And even though I have to face the prospect of being a minority of one, I humbly believe I have the courage to be in such a hopeless minority.' Mahatma Gandhi (2 March, 1922)

79 'Injustice anywhere is a threat to justice everywhere. We are caught in an inescapable network of mutuality, tied in a single garment of destiny. Whatever affects one directly, affects all indirectly.' Martin Luther King, Jr. (16 April 1963)

80 'Well, Doctor, what have we got – a Republic or a Monarchy?' 'A Republic – if you can keep it.' Benjamin Franklin (1787) [We are still waiting on this one...]

Five websites

81 Freedom House: http://www.freedomhouse.org/

82 Partners for Democratic Change: http://www.partnersglobal.org/

83 UN Human Rights page: http://www.un.org/en/rights/

84 National Endowment for Democracy (USA): http://www.ned.org/

85 http://www.dailykos.com/story/2011/11/20/1038188/-Fiscal-inequality-Godzilla-vs-Ants. One of the best explanations I have seen of the pernicious effect on political democracy of gross economic inequality.

Five things you can do as a democratic citizen

86 Pay attention. Read reliable media sources – critically. Don't believe something just because it suits your viewpoint (tempting though that is).

87 Get involved – for instance in local, employee or student politics. Some social contexts have more opportunities to participate on a local level than others, but make the most of those that present themselves. One central opportunity/ duty in many democracies, which should be embraced, is serving as a juror. Only through participation can you really *practise* democracy.

88 Join a public interest group, NGO or, *preferably*, a political party that approximates your own political (and moral) beliefs and goals – because power in a democracy is still best articulated through parties.

89 Find a forum of debate. Express your opinions by writing to media outlets, blogging or using social media networks. Discussions of political issues among friends or colleagues, or in the pub or coffeehouse, also count, but might not be so coherent. Attend – or organize – political events such as meetings, marches and demonstrations. Peaceful, law-abiding protest is part of the essence of democracy.

90 Take action. Democracy is a matter of practice more than contemplation: join a political campaign, when they come around; help out the political causes you believe in with your time, money, or both; if you think you have more to contribute, run for elected office.

Four freedoms

This (liberal) democratic quartet originated in the State of the Union speech of President Franklin Delano Roosevelt on 6 January 1941. The four freedoms were later incorporated in the agreed Anglo-American war aims, summed up in the Atlantic Charter of August 1941, and eventually the Universal Declaration of Human Rights of 1948. The freedoms are:

91 Freedom of speech

92 Freedom of worship

93 Freedom from want

94 Freedom from fear

The first two were standards of American constitutionalism. Freedom from want and fear, however, were new and, for many, controversial. They were the basis for the ensuing claim to an individual right to economic 'human security', and for the call for a system of international conflict prevention, which resulted in the United Nations system. The most radical aspect of the quartet was, perhaps, that they could be applied universally to all humanity, on an international level that overrode national or state sovereignty.

Three aspects of democracy

95 Liberty

96 Equality

97 Fraternity

The French Revolution of 1789 was in practice a disaster for modern democracy, but in theory it was an immense success. The revolutionary triad remains a key way of understanding the complex balancing act that modern democracy remains, between the wish to preserve and empower individual freedom on the one hand, and the need to retain a basic equality (of whatever form) within the polis between its members; this, and the fact that the best, perhaps only, way to achieve this balance is by providing the binding element *between* citizens – 'fraternity', a concept that suggests much more than just brotherhood. The basis of this fraternity then happens to be the understanding through the experience of democratic practice that neither liberty nor equality can survive in a polis without the other principle. Democratic fraternity is the mutual interdependence of the free and the equal.

Two concepts of liberty

98 Negative freedom (freedom from)

99 Positive freedom (freedom to)

We usually see these as antagonists: when we keep the state *from* having power over us as individuals (negative freedom), we are also preventing ourselves as a collective (the state) having the power *to* do something that is to our overall benefit, and vice versa. But the two freedoms, when given appropriate roles, can also be seen as co-dependent parts of a vital democracy. It has often been the (democratic) state's role, through the exercise of positive freedom, to preserve the negative freedom of some from the depredations and persecution of other citizens (and other parts of the polity). The federal government's role in the American civil rights struggle of the 1950s and 1960s is an example.

Note: the 'freedom *from* want' and 'freedom *from* fear' of the 'four freedoms', expressed in terms of negative freedom, cannot be upheld unless we as a democracy have the positive freedom *to* organize a social safety net (involving taxation) and *to* provide for external and internal security, even involving co-operation in international multilateral organizations to prevent national aggression the world over. Hence the welfare state and the United Nations can both be based on concepts of *negative* freedom.

One person, one vote

100 Participate. If you are over 18, you are, with few exceptions, a full stakeholder in your democracy. Exercise your democratic rights and responsibilities – and vote.

Index

abuse of power 69
activism 85–6
aleatory democracy 19
American democracy 8–10
American Revolution 35–6, 38, 42
anti-state *vs.* pro-state 89–93
Arab Spring 3–4, 5–6, 110–12
Argentina 112
aristocracy 83
aristocratic republics 31–2
Aristotle 28
Articles of Confederation 35
Asia 114–16
Athenian democracy 19, 26, 27–9
Australia 49
Austria 40, 48, 49, 54, 83, 117

Bagehot, Walter 48
banyan democracy 19
Berlin, Isaiah 55, 66–7
Berlusconi, Silvio 87, 88
bicameral legislature 69
Bill of Rights 42
Bonaparte, Napoleon 43
Brazil 10, 76, 100, 112
Britain 45, 49, 60, 70–1, 80, 82
bureaucracy 90
Burke, Edmund 42
Bush, George W. 81

capitalism 54
central banks 73
Chartist movement 48
check and balances 69
China 10–11, 61, 106, 114–15, 127, 128
Christian democracy 20, 129–30
Churchill, Winston 12, 60, 126

city-states 31, 32, 38
civic nationalism 56
civil liberties 118–20
Civil Rights campaign 62
civil service 70, 90
civil societies 46, 53, 64, 72–3
Civil War 34–5
climate change 126–7
coalitions 82–3
Commonwealth regime 34
communism 3, 11, 52, 59, 61, 127, 128
community 53–5
Community acquis 17
Community of Democracies 4, 14–15
complacency, unwarranted 5–10
components, of democracy 14–17, 27
Constitution of the United States of America 35–6, 42
constitutions 69
Corn Laws 46
Council of Constance (1414–18) 34
coventanters' movement 41
Crick, Bernard 24, 74
Cuba 113

Dahl, Robert A. 16
Darwinism 56
Declaration of Independence 42
Declaration of the Rights of Man and of the Citizen 42
definition, of democracy 14
Democracy Index 4, 5, 15, 113
democratic deficit 84–6
democratic revolutions 35–6
Democrats 8–9
direct democracy 18

discrimination 56
diversity 55–6, 118

Economist Intelligence Unit 4, 15
education 73
Egypt 6, 111
electoral reform 46
electoral systems 16–17, 70–2, 80–3
11 September 2011 (terrorist attack) 8
England 32, 34–5, 39, 41, 45–6
enlightened absolutism 40, 43
equality 24, 39–40, 42, 75–6
estate assemblies 34
estates 40
ethnonationalism 57, 99
euro crisis 7–8
Europe 47–8, 116–17
European Union 7–8, 17, 63, 64, 77,
    100–4

fascism 52, 59, 60, 127
federal democracy 19, 100
feudal system 33
financial crisis 7–8, 64, 91–2
financial discipline 122
Finland 49
flawed democracies 4, 113
flaws 80–4
Florence 32
France 35, 40, 49, 71, 99
free market 44–7, 73
freedom 22–4, 40–1, 66–7
Freedom House 4, 5, 15
French Revolution 36, 38, 42–3

Gallie, W.B. 75
gender equality 46, 130–1
Germany 7–8, 16, 33, 38, 49, 54, 57,
    60, 64, 98–100, 117
gerrymandering 84

Gettysburg address 14
global democratization 3–4, 77,
    96–107
good governance 70
governmental models 10–12
governmental structure 68–70
'great divergence' 86
Great Slump 59
Greek democracy (ancient) 18, 19,
    26, 27–9
Grote, George 28

Hanseatic League 31
Hegel, G.W.F. 97
Herder, Johann Gottfried 57
Herzl, Theodor 132
Hirschman, Albert O. 76
Hitler, Adolf 59
Hobbes, Thomas 39
human rights 17, 61, 106
Hungary 8, 33, 49, 116–17

India 10, 55, 61, 76,
    100, 114
Indonesia 10, 100
Industrial Revolution 45
inequality 23–4,
    53, 80–3
Internet 118–21
Ireland 7
irredentism 58
Islam 10, 30, 111–12, 130–1
Islamophobia 118
Italy 7, 31, 32, 38, 57, 59

Japan 99
Jim Crow laws 52
Joseph II 40
judicial branch of government
    69–70

Kant, Immanuel 97
Keynesianism 117
King, Martin Luther 62
King, Rodney 66
kingship 32–3

Labour Party 54
Latin America 43–4
Léon of Spain 33
Levellers 41
Leviathan 39
liberal democracy 18, 21–4, 47–9
liberal pluralism 55
liberalism 22
liberty 40–1, 42
Lincoln, Abraham 14
local democracy 19
Locke, John 41
Los Angeles Riots 66
lower-classes 53–4
loyalty 76
Lutheranism 39

Machiavelli, Niccolò 32
Madison, James 14, 55
Magna Carta 33, 38
market democracy 21–4
market economy 54, 128
Marshall, John 36
Marsiglio of Padua 31
Marx, Karl 22, 54
Mazzini, Guiseppe 58
McCarthyism 61
measurement, of democracy 4–5, 15
media outlets 87–8, 118
Mexico 113
middle classes 45, 47, 48
Mill, John Stuart 46, 48
monitory democracy 19
Montesquieu 35
Muslim society 30, 100

Napoleonic Code 43
nation-states 76–7, 96–101
National Covenant 41
national identity 98–100
National Socialist Party 59, 60
national unification 57
nationalism 56–9, 63–4, 89
negative freedom 66–7
neoliberal position 66
Netherlands 100
New Deal 60
new technology 118–21
New Zealand 49
NGOs (non-governmental
      organizations) 64, 72
Nietzsche, Friedrich 55–6
non-democratic models 10–12
Norway 49

Obama, Barrack 8, 9, 64, 85, 92, 126
oligarchy 24, 83–4
On Liberty 48
origin, of democracy 26–30

Pakistan 61
parliamentary democracy 19, 68–9
parliaments 32–3, 34–5
participation 84–6
participatory democracy 19
People's Republic of China *see* China
Plato 28
pluralism 62–3, 99
pluralist democracy 19, 24
plurality voting 70–1, 82
plutocracy 7, 24
Poland 33, 34, 60
political parties 72
politics 73–5
the Pope 34
Popper, Karl 55
Portugal 7

positive freedom 66–7
post-Cold War 64
power, abuse of 69
presidential democracy 68–9
proportional representation (PR) 70,
    71, 83

racist policies 61–2
Reform Bill 45–6
religion and democracy 128–31
representative democracies 18–19,
    26, 32–5, 80–3, 100
Republicans 8–10, 92
republics 31–2
revolutions 35–6
right-wing agenda 89–93
Roman Republic 31–2
Roosevelt, Franklin Delano 60
Rothschild, Anselm 48
rule of law 38
Russia 4–5, 11, 59, 64, 106, 116

Saudi Arabia 11, 112
Scandinavian countries 49, 99
Schelling, Thomas 131
Scotland 41, 71
Second World War 59–60
secular democracy 20–1, 130
self-government 26, 30–2, 67–8
Senate 70
Singapore 11, 114
Skinner, Quentin 38
slavery 27–8, 47
Smith, Adam 45
social democracy 24
social justice 63
social mobility 86
social welfare programmes 54, 89
socialism 53–5
Socrates 28
South Africa 76, 113

South America 112–13
sovereignty 39, 64, 77
Soviet Union 61
Spain 7
spread, of democracy 3–4
Sub-Saharan Africa 113–14
suffrage 46, 47, 48–9, 53
Supreme Court 36, 42, 69
surveillance 118–19
Swiss assemblies 30
Switzerland 49, 76, 99
Syria 6, 111–12

Taylor, A.J.P 110
Tea Party 10, 85, 92
terrorism 8, 118
Thatcher, Margaret 71
theocracy 128–9
theory of democracy 66
theory of salience 131–2
Third Estate 40
Thomas Aquinas 41
threats to democracy
    118–20
Tocqueville, Alexis de 44,
    46–7, 86
transparency 70
Turkey 10, 111
tyranny 22–3

unions 53
United Kingdom 99
United Nations (UN) 64, 104–7
Universal Declaration of Human
    Rights 61
universal suffrage 48–9
USA (United States of America) 8–10,
    18, 35–6, 42, 44, 47, 60, 61–2,
    63–4, 70–1, 76, 81–2, 86, 91–2,
    99, 126
Utilitarianism 46

Venetian republic 31
veto power 105
Voltaire 35
voting 70–2, 80–3

wealth, and power 87–9, 122
The Wealth of Nations 45
Westphalian state 39
women 46, 48, 58, 106, 130

Acknowledgements

The author would like to thank personally the many individuals whose patience and acumen helped shape the views expressed in this book. Bill Friend, David Ruffin and Erik Willenz were kind enough to read the original draft. The other Friday group members were also most helpful, even when in disagreement. Of others further afield, Allan Janik, Peter Pulzer, Ivar Oxaal, Edmund Leites, Mitchell Cohen, Jan and Herta Palme, Richard Tuck, Norman Stone and Tim Blanning deserve particular thanks for their views, inspiration and encouragement. Mickey Beller was ever my strongest and dearest critic, Andrew Brimmer always an exemplar of the practice of agreeing to disagree most agreeably, as is Doris Brimmer. Esther Diane Brimmer has done more than anyone to help me write this book – except perhaps for Hermi Beller, from whom I learned, in her own quiet way, more about democracy than anyone else. I hope I have as good an influence on Nathaniel Brimmer-Beller, whom I also thank for his many insights, as my mother did on me. This book is dedicated to her memory, and to my son's education as a citizen.

The publisher and author would like to express their thanks for permission to reproduce the following images: **Chapter 1:** Tahrir Square demonstration © Hang Dinh/Shutterstock.com **Chapter 2:** Eleanor Roosevelt – Material obtained on 17/07/2013 from the website of the United Nations Audiovisual Library of International Law, located at http://www.un.org/law/avl Copyright © United Nations, 2008 **Chapter 3:** The Pnyx © Dmitri Kessel//Time Life Pictures/Getty Images **Chapter 5:** Martin Luther King © Roger-Viollet/Rex Features **Chapter 7:** Sergio Berlusconi © miqu77/Shutterstock.com **Chapter 8:** European Parliament © AND Inc/Shutterstock.com **Chapter 9:** 'Goddess of Democracy' © Peter Turnley/CORBIS